J Bishop

Heart Melodies of an Aged Pilgrim

J Bishop

Heart Melodies of an Aged Pilgrim

ISBN/EAN: 9783744729130

Printed in Europe, USA, Canada, Australia, Japan

Cover: Foto ©Lupo / pixelio.de

More available books at **www.hansebooks.com**

HEART MELODIES

OF

AN AGED PILGRIM.

BY THE

AUTHOR OF "ONLY A SERVANT."

"Speaking to yourselves in psalms and hymns and spiritual songs, singing and making melody in your heart to the Lord."
EPH. v. 19.

Edinburgh:
ANDREW STEVENSON,
1891.

PREFACE.

WHAT the Author says in the note prefixed to the verses entitled "The Ever Living Saviour" (*vide* page 67), may be applied to the whole contents of this little book. He can "lay no claim to originality either in the thought or expression" of his verses, and would not presume to call his simple rhymes poetry. He has but gathered some precious pearls from the vast ocean of God's revealed Word, in the shape of those truths which are fitted to convey hope, comfort, and consolation to weary pilgrims on their journey Zionward, and strung them together in a form which, it may be, meets the apostolical injunction that we should make melody in our hearts to the Lord.

Most of the pieces have been written after the close of a busy business career of perhaps more than ordinary length; the greater part of them indeed, during the "borrowed years" that succeed the allotted threescore and ten; and in those wakeful hours when impaired health interfered with his enjoyment of "tired nature's sweet restorer—balmy sleep."

At such seasons it was a calming and grateful occupation to turn the thoughts of the unduly active mind in the direction of the things that belong to our everlasting peace; and he trusts his little volume may be found useful in the case of others, as its contents have often been in his own, in bringing a peaceful quiet and refreshing into these oft-times otherwise painful hours.

He regrets that he is unable to give any indication to the authorship of the lines given on page 132—"To a Mother on the Death of her First-born Son." They are of such a date as to make it certain that he has not been infringing any one's copyright; and their merit is such as cannot fail to make them acceptable to the readers of what might prove an otherwise disappointing volume. They have been inserted here mainly as a specimen and record of an unwonted feat of memory on the part of an affectionate sister, such as he believes is not often paralleled. B.

BRUNTSFIELD PLACE,
   EDINBURGH.

CONTENTS.

	PAGE
AGED PILGRIM'S SOLILOQUY, THE,	111
ALL-SUFFICIENT SAVIOUR, THE,	151
ASPIRATIONS,	138
BAIRNS' HYMN, A,	146
BEREAVED, TO THE: A HYMN OF CONSOLATION,	18
BEULAH,	41
COMPASSIONATE SAVIOUR, THE,	148
DEATH-BED EXPERIENCE, A,	142
DEATH ENCOUNTERED,	58
"DID NOT I SEE THEE IN THE GARDEN WITH HIM?"	51
DISCIPLESHIP,	64
"DO YOU LOVE GOD?"	90
EVER-LIVING SAVIOUR, THE,	67
FAINT AND WEARY,	154
FLIGHT OF TIME, THE,	118
GIFTS OF GRACE, THE,	107
GOD'S HOUSE ON EARTH,	160
GOD IN NATURE AND IN GRACE,	121
GOSPEL FEAST, THE,	45
"I HAVE PRAYED FOR THEE THAT THY FAITH FAIL NOT,"	33

CONTENTS.

IN MEMORIAM—MARY H——: ONLY A SERVANT,	100
IN MEMORIAM—MARY J. NICHOL, SECRETARY OF THE INVALIDS' AUXILIARY TO THE EDINBURGH MEDICAL MISSIONARY SOCIETY,	23
"I WILL IN NO WISE CAST OUT,"	157
OLD BETTY,	78
OPENED EYE, THE,	73
PARABLE, A,	14
PERFECT GOD AND PERFECT MAN,	55
POOR NELL,	29
PRAYER, A,	49
RELEASED,	11
REMINISCENCES,	129
RESPITED,	1
RESTORED,	86
RETROSPECTION,	113
REVIVED,	5
SABBATH, THE,	38
SALVATION'S STORY,	89
SUSTAINED,	8
TELL THE STORY FAR AND WIDE,	26
WILLING TO DEPART,	76

RESPITED.

"Thou hast in love to my soul delivered it from the pit. . . . For the grave cannot praise Thee, death can not celebrate Thee. . . . The living, the living, he shall praise Thee, as I do this day."—ISA. xxxviii. 17-19.

HE has brought me back from the border land—
    From the very gates of death—
Where I felt the touch of Death's clammy hand,
    And the chill of his icy breath.

He has given me back to your earnest prayers,
    O friends, most loved and true!
He has seen you were loath from me to part—
    He has work for me still to do.

And I gladly stay, since such is His will,
    For He knows what's best for me—
If He keeps me here—if He calls me hence—
    It is still with Himself to be.

I would sit, like Mary, at His feet,
    Or, like John, lean on His breast;
I would take up my cross and follow Him,
    And would seek no other rest

Than the rest that is found in working for Him—
    It may be a soul to win—
A word to speak to some sorrowing one,
    Or a sinner to guide to Him:

Or it may be only to suffer awhile,
    To show what His grace can do,
And that what you see of His work in me
    May strengthen and comfort you.

I would never forget His love to me,
    But would tell it again and again—
How He filled my soul with cloudless peace,
    When my body was racked with pain;

How I fed on His precious promises,
    And was kept in perfect peace,
When I thought of my own unworthiness,
    And of His abundant grace.

I scarce could claim to be counted His child,
    For I knew how wayward I'd been,
And aught as His servant I'd sought to do
    Had always been tainted with sin.

So I felt that only the sinner's place
    Was the place to be taken by me;
And that was enough for me, dear Lord!
    For the sinner is welcomed by Thee.

As such it is that we come to Thee,
    Having nought of our own to plead;
But Thy perfect life and Thy precious blood
    Are made ours by the Father's deed.

For He loved the lost with a boundless love,
    When He saw them dead in sin;
And He gave His Son to take our place,
    And made us complete in Him.

And now having nought of our own to boast,
    We look for our all to Thee;
We cling to Thy cross, and we trust in Thy word,
    And we find Thou hast made us free;

Free from the love and the guilt of sin,
    From the law's condemning power,
From the pride of life, from the fear of death,
    And from him who seeks to devour.

And so we go on in our pilgrim way,
    Committing our all to Thee,
And we find Thy grace is enough for us here,
    And enough for Eternity!

REVIVED.

"Though I walk through the valley of the shadow of death, I will fear no evil: for Thou art with me; Thy rod and Thy staff they comfort me."—Ps. xxiii. 4.

TRUST Thee, Saviour! yes, I'll trust Thee,
    Trust Thee, though I cannot see—
Thine it is to choose my pathway—
    Mine is but to follow Thee.

Let the way be bright or dreary,
    Smooth or rough the path I tread,
All is well when Thou art near me,
    Telling me by whom I'm led.

Though I know not what's before me,
    All the way is plain to Thee,
Every turning, every winding,
    Few or many as they be.

Let me but enjoy Thy presence,
    That will brighten all the way ;
And the morning, gilt with promise,
    Will bring in the perfect day.

For I know at least the ending—
    That my faith reveals to me—
Rest and peace and joy eternal,
    Given and made sure by Thee.

Rest and peace and joy, what blessing !
    Rest from travail, toil, and pain ;
Peace from fear and doubt and fighting,
    Every foe o'ercome and slain.

And such joy, so pure and holy,
    As in heaven alone could be,
That same joy, O precious Saviour !
    Which is in and flows from Thee.

So I press on in my journey,
    Casting on Thee all my care,
Sure Thou never wilt forsake me,
    But will still my burdens bear.

Yes, Thy grace will still support me,
    Fit for glory day by day,
Till made perfect in Thine image,
    Thou wilt call me hence away;

Away from time and all its sorrow,
    Sin and suffering, shame and pain;
Away from earth and imperfection,
    Heaven and all its bliss to gain.

SUSTAINED.

"Thou shalt call His name JESUS: for He shall save His people from their sins."—MATT. i. 21.

"Thy name is as ointment poured forth."—CANT. i. 3.

I STOOD by the bed of the dying one,
   And sought to uphold her hope and faith;
Her pilgrim race was nearly run,
   And she lay there, face to face with death.

I spoke of the names of our blessed Lord,
   So fitted to comfort, to cheer, and sustain,
And I thought that "Immanuel—God with us,"
   Would soothe her, lying there racked with pain.

I said that in each of His glorious names
   Some trait of His wondrous grace is expressed;
"Oh, yes," she replied, with a happy smile,
   "But I like His name of 'JESUS' best."

Yes, Jesus, Thy name to the sinner is dear,
    For it speaks of the ransom fully paid,
Of the stains washed out, of the sin subdued,
    And the filthy one all comely made.

Of our sins it speaks and Thy righteousness,
    Of the shame and the pain which Thou didst bear,
And the glorious robe, so pure and white,
    Wrought out by Thee for Thine own to wear.

It tells of life to the dead in sin,
    Of strength to the weak and feeble one,
Of refuge from wrath and escape from hell,
    And of heaven with all its joys begun.

It tells of Satan o'erthrown and foiled,
    Of Jehovah honoured and glorified,
Of mercy in copious streams outpoured,
    And justice appeased and satisfied;

Of the FATHER'S love and the SPIRIT'S aid,
    Of all we need laid up in the SON—
The THREE COMBINED to give grace while here,
    And glory at last when time is gone.

Do we wonder then she rejoiced in this name,
   And prized it when passing on to her rest?
No, we feel we would rather with her say,
   We, too, like His name of "JESUS" best!

RELEASED.

"Lord Jesus, receive my spirit. . . . And when he had said this, he fell asleep."—ACTS vii. 59, 60.

SHE is passing away,
    For her call has come;
And the Master now
    Is leading her home.

The road may seem rough—
    'Tis the same that He trod—
And she feels it enough
    That she be as her Lord.

His presence is with her,
    To uphold and to cheer;
With His arms underneath her
    She has nothing to fear.

She is kept on the Rock,
    Still trusting His word,—
For langour and pain
    Soon the joy of her Lord.

Her dark night of weeping
    Will ere long be o'er,
For the morning of joy
    Casts its bright beams before.

The gates stand ajar
    At the end of the way:
Even now she sees gleams
    Of eternal day.

The angels are waiting
    To usher her in,—
One more of His ransomed
    From death and from sin.

Her loved ones are round her,
    Her passing to cheer;
So bright is her prospect,
    They can't keep her here.

Oh, no, though the parting
    Brings sorrow and pain,
They're cheered by the hope
    Of soon meeting again,

Where the loved gone before
    In expectancy stand,
To welcome her home
    To Immanuel's land.

'Tis enough, righteous Father!
    Let Thy will be done!
Farewell now to earth,
    Heaven's bliss is begun!

A PARABLE.

"All these things are against me."—GEN. xlii. 36.

"We know that all things work together for good to them that love God."—ROM. viii. 28.

"THE journey is so very long, and so weary is the way,
Oh, when will ever we get home?" we're often heard to say.
"They stop at every station, thus losing so much time;
When will we reach the terminus of this tiresome railway line?

"We're shut up here so cramped for room, and so comfortless the seat,
We've got no cushions to our backs, nor warmers for our feet,

These broken windows have no screens, and to make the thing complete,
How rude and disagreeable are the passengers we meet!"

Alas! how many passengers are found in every train
Who constantly thus grumble, and do nothing but complain;
While if they'd only think a bit, examining their pass,
They'd find they'd got, by their own fault, into another class

Of carriage than they should be in, and they're alone to blame;
The Master came to see them off, and booked them in His name,
He bought the tickets at the bar, all cost to them to save,
And had they only looked they'd seen 'twas a first class one He gave.

O Christian! does this parable no lesson bear for
    thee?
Do not you in this passenger your own true picture
    see?
Your Father has provided you all blessings for the
    way,
But, oh, how oft you walk by sense, and let unbelief
    have sway!
Need you wonder then if comfort leaves, and your
    peace is ta'en away?

You should not go with downcast look, complaining
    of your lot,
Nor harbour thoughts of discontent, as if your Lord
    had not
Remembered all He undertook, when first He
    rescued you
From fearful pit and miry clay. Is not His promise
    true?
Be sure the work His grace began shall be accom-
    plished too.

And has He not, oft in times past, such blessings
    on you poured,

That well He merits at your hands to be for aye
    adored,
As your bountiful Provider, Protector, Leader,
    Guide?
He gave His Son to save your soul, can there be
    aught beside,
In earth below or heaven above, that He will not
    provide?

You must not think you will not meet some trials
    by the way,
'Twont do to have the sun aye shine and keep the
    clouds away;
We need the rain, the wind, the frost, to fertilise
    the ground,
Without these in their seasons due no autumn
    fruit is found.

And if the Christian, too, would grow, and be at last
    complete,
He seeks the footsteps of his Lord, and there he
    plants his feet
In the prints the Man of Sorrows left in the painful
    path He trod,
And in fellowship in suffering gets closer to his God.

TO THE BEREAVED.

A HYMN OF CONSOLATION.

These verses have already been published and circulated as a leaflet.

"Blessed be God, even the Father of our Lord Jesus Christ, the Father of mercies, and the God of all comfort, who comforteth us in all our tribulation, that we may be able to comfort them which are in any trouble, by the comfort wherewith we ourselves are comforted of God."—2 COR. i. 3, 4.

"Wherefore comfort one another with these words."—1 THESS. iv. 18.

THEY are gathering fast in the home above—
    The friends we have known and loved below;
We shall miss them here, but they're welcomed there,
    Then why should we grieve to let them go?

We shall miss them here? Nay, Memory still
    Will ofttimes bring them back to our view;

We'll hear them speak, and we'll speak to them,
    And we'll live all our happy past anew.

We will find them again when we meet with their friends—
    And again when we kneel at the throne of grace,
We will meet them there at our Saviour's feet,
    And rejoice with them at that Resting place.

They'll be here when we look on the scenes they loved—
    When we read their favourite books once more;
And the words they spake and the things they did
    Will seem more real than they did before.

We'll hear their voice in the household psalm,
    When we gather together to praise the Lord,
And to drink again of the healing springs
    From the rich deep well of His Holy word.

They'll go with us again to the house of God,
    And we'll take sweet counsel as we go,
And our hearts will burn as we talk by the way,
    And bring back the bright Sabbaths of long ago.

And oh, if Memory thus hallows the past,
    And brings what we most loved back again!
What shall we say of what faith reveals
    Of the bliss they have gained and we pant to gain?

"Father, I will," the Saviour hath said,
    "That those Thou hast given Me be with Me here."
WITH CHRIST! CAUGHT UP BY HIS OWN DESIRE!
    Oh, who would not wish to be welcomed there?

They have left behind them their sin-stained dress;
    They have finished their course and kept the faith,
And now, through their Saviour's righteousness,
    They are freed from sin and have conquered Death.

They have reached the abode prepared for them,
    The home they had ever kept in view;
And the joys which they find in that Resting place
    They longingly wait to share with you.

There's no taint of sin there, and no touch of pain—
    No sorrow to grieve, and no care to annoy—
For as all are made perfect in holiness,
    So all are made perfect in love and joy.

It would baffle an angel's tongue to express
    All the joy of that pure and peaceful abode;
Who can say what it is to behold the Lord's face?
    Who can say what it is to be EVER WITH GOD?

But the Lamb Himself is the light thereof,
    And all who are there His likeness bear—
WITH HIM AND WITH THEM IN THAT RESTING
    PLACE!
    Oh, who would not wish to be welcomed there?

'Tis the Saviour's will that keeps us here,
    Even that same will that called them home;
So we'll patiently wait His appointed time,
    And be ready to go when He bids us come.

We will take up the work which they have laid down,
    And it may be we'll reap of that they have sowed;

Into their loved labours we'll enter here—
   We'll rejoice with them there in the joy of their God.

At a distance still from our Father's house,
   A little longer our cross we must bear—
In a "little while" His call will come,
   And THEY'LL BE AMONG THOSE WHO WILL WELCOME US THERE!

These lines, with their accompanying note, were sent by the writer to the widow of a much loved friend, on the occasion of her husband's death. Bereavement is the common lot of all, and what proves consolatory to one wounded heart may prove equally so to others. They have therefore been revised, and are now cast on the waters, with a prayer to the God of all comfort, that He may be pleased to use them for blessing to His afflicted ones in their dark and cloudy day.

MY DEAR MRS. ——

        My thoughts, which have been much with you since Monday morning, have found expression in the accompanying lines, which I now send to you, in the hope of their imparting to you some of that comfort wherewith I myself have been comforted of God. May they be blessed for this end of Him who is the God of all comfort. To Him I commend you, and with heartfelt sympathy, I remain yours most sincerely,   J. B. B.

IN MEMORIAM

Mary J. Nichol, for many years the active and energetic Secretary of the Invalids' Auxiliary to the Edinburgh Medical Missionary Society, who died at Bridge of Allan, on 6th June 1890.

"Well done, good and faithful servant: . . . enter thou into the joy of thy Lord."—Matt. xxv. 23.

Happy spirit, now released
    From thy suffering and thy pain;
Welcomed home to endless bliss,
    To an everlasting reign!

Weary days and sleepless nights
    Were thy portion here below,
Aching limbs and palsied frame,
    Feverish tossings to and fro.

"Twas the way the Master trod,
    And the way He chose for thee,
That thy sufferings might be used
    To show how rich His grace could be.

But the suffering now is ended,
    And the glory has begun;
Now thy well-fought fight is over,
    And the heavenly prize is won!

He was with thee in the furnace,
    Giving grace and strength to bear—
Thou art with Him now in glory,
    All His promised bliss to share.

Thy bright crown, so rich with jewels
    Gathered for Him here below
By thy work and witness for Him—
    How it shines upon thy brow!

For the work thine own hands fashioned,
    Gladly though 'twas wrought by thee,
Was not all thy service rendered—
    No, how many now there be,

Winningly by thee enlisted,
    Willingly their part to bear
In the blessed work of mercy,
    Ever to thyself so dear.

And how many a suffering sick one
    Learned from thee that even they
(In their helplessness and weakness,
    Thinking they could only pray)

Could do something for the Master,
    Something He would reckon good,
Something which would gain His verdict—
    That she had done what she could.

Some of them are home already,
    Sharing with thee in His joy;
Some have caught thy fallen mantle,
    Work like thine their loved employ.

And aloft the banner waving,
    On they follow as did'st thou,
Cheered still by thy bright example,
    And the thought of what thou'rt now!

TELL THE STORY FAR AND WIDE.

"How beautiful upon the mountains are the feet of him that bringeth good tidings, that publisheth peace; that bringeth good tidings of good, that publisheth salvation; that saith unto Zion, Thy God reigneth."—Isa. lii. 7.

Tell the story far and wide,
    Tell it o'er and o'er again
Tell what mercy doth provide,
    Rebel hearts like ours to gain.

Tell the story far and wide,
    Tell it o'er and o'er again—
A victim to the altar led,
    The Lamb of God for sinners slain.

Tell the story far and wide,
    Tell it o'er and o'er again—
Jesus Christ is crucified,
    God is reconciled to men.

Tell the story far and wide.
  Tell it o'er and o'er again—
Justice now is satisfied,
  Sin atoned, and left no stain.

Tell the story far and wide,
  Tell it o'er and o'er again—
Jesus Christ is glorified,
  And He comes as King to reign.

Tell the story far and wide,
  Tell it o'er and o'er again—
Now the gospel banquet's spread,
  Costly viands, choicest wine.

Tell the story far and wide,
  Tell it o'er and o'er again—
Christ's Himself the living bread,
  Giving health and life to men.

Tell the story far and wide,
  Tell it o'er and o'er again—
Hear the Spirit and the Bride
  Calling—Shall they call in vain?

Tell the story far and wide,
    Tell it o'er and o'er again---
All may come, for all are bid,
    All may freely enter in.

POOR NELL.

"I am sought of them that asked not for Me; I am found of them that sought Me not."—Isa. lxv. 1.

"Jesus called them unto Him, and said, Suffer little children to come unto Me, and forbid them not: for of such is the kingdom of God."—Luke xviii. 16.

DARK lowered the wintry sky,
 And the rain in torrents fell,
The biting winds were high,
 When poor little ragged Nell,

While she struggled against the storm,
 Chanced, as she ran, to espy
A room, oh, so bright and so warm,
 And so pleasing to the eye!

The fire in the well-filled grate
  Sent its beams across the way,
And told of the welcome heat
  It gave out on that stormy day.

And glad children went trooping in—
  Nell heard their happy song—
And the teacher looked so good and kind,
  As he stood 'mid the happy throng.

The contrast was so great,
  'Twixt the cheerful scene within,
And the cold and cheerless street—
  She could not but wish to be in.

But the children, as in they passed,
  Were all tidy and neat and clean,
And she was a ragged lass,
  Her clothes tattered and torn and mean.

Yet she thought of the kindly look
  That beamed on the teacher's face,
As he welcomed each little one in,
  So she plucked up heart of grace,

And when next the door was opened
    To let more of the children through,
She ran and she thus addressed him,
    Ere he from the door withdrew—

"Please, Sir, I'm a poor little creature,
    My clothes neither tidy nor clean,
But you seem so kind, may I ask, Sir,
    If the likes of me may come in?"

The teacher had learned of the Master,
    And he thought of the words He had given,
"Let the little ones come unto Me,
    For of such is the kingdom of heaven."

His heart and his eyes too were full
    As he looked on poor Nell, and he smiled;
While she joyed as she heard his reply,
    "You are heartily welcome, my child."

So he took the poor wanderer in,
    And near the fire gave her a place,
Where the wet garments soon became drier,
    And happiness lit up her face.

While the little ones gather around,
  Each with a sweet welcome prepared
For this other poor child who had found
  The shelter that long they had shared.

There was joy at that hour, too, in heaven,
  'Midst the angels and saints above,
O'er this poor little waif who had found
  Her way to the Lord whom they love.

"I HAVE PRAYED FOR THEE, THAT THY FAITH FAIL NOT."

"Ye are all the children of God by faith in Christ Jesus."—GAL. iii. 26. "Justified by faith."—ROM. v. 1. "Precious faith."—2 PET. i. 1. "Worketh by love."—GAL. v. 6. "Purifying their hearts by faith."—ACTS xv. 9. "Overcometh the world."—1 JOHN v. 4.

"Receiving the end of your faith, even the salvation of your souls."—1 PET. i. 9.

"And what shall I more say? for the time would fail me to tell."—HEB. xi. 32.

AH, Peter!—confident and vain—
Thou'rt in the tempter's toils again!
And hid from thy pride-blinded eyes
Is all that now before thee lies—

The fierce assault, the sad defeat,
The base denial, and complete
Forsaking, followed, as was meet,
By bitter oaths and shameless lies—
All these are hidden from thine eyes.

But He, whose eye can all things see
Of past, or present, or to be,
Hath seen it all, and well doth know
The working of that crafty foe,
Who now through thee another blow
Aims at Himself, in this the hour
Of darkness and of Satan's power,
Raised up against Him. Yet, for thee,
Even in His own extremity,
He feels and prays. The raging crowd
Surrounds Him, thirsting for His blood.
He knows His Father at His cry
Would send the angel-hosts from high
To save; yet would He not go free.
He prays,—but Simon, 'tis for thee!

O weary sinner, bending low
Beneath the tempter's bitter blow,

And feeling that with such a foe
'Tis vain for feeble thee to cope ;
Hear the sweet words of heavenly hope—
Faint not, for in that evil hour,
However dark that hour may be,
Thy very weakness brings the power
That lifts thee up, and rescues thee.
For He, who ever intercedes
Before the throne, for thee now pleads,
And 'tis an all-prevailing plea
Thy Saviour there presents for thee!

What asked He for the tempted one
Whose boasted courage now was gone?
That angel legions might be sent
To save him? Or at least prevent
The sad denial? Or that He
Who erst in dark Gethsemane
The bloody sweat wiped from His brow
Would re-appear—His errand now
To cheer the lowly servant, and afford
Strength unto him, as erewhile to his Lord?
Not such His prayers.

What was it then
He pleaded for? Oh, hear again
Another witness from the lips divine,
Who gives His testimony line on line,
To thy prevailing power, O precious Faith!
That overcomes the world and conquers death!
He only asks that, when the foes assail
And lay His followers low, thou should'st not fail!

Hail, precious Faith! Oh, who can tell
The virtue that in thee doth dwell?
Thou art the eye by which we see
Jehovah's long hid mystery.
Through thee we learn His gracious plan
For justifying sinful man.
Nay more, the eye but gives us sight,
And brings this wondrous plan to light;
But thou'rt the hand by which we take
Boons freely given for Jesus' sake,
And pardon, peace, and righteousness,
And love, and joy through thee possess.
Thou break'st the chains in which we're led,
And link'st us to our living Head.

And thou'rt the mouth by which we feed
On Him, and find Him meat indeed ;
By thee from death to life we rise ;
By thee the simple are made wise ;
The weak made strong; all rich supplies
The poor receive, their portion here
Is God Himself, and Paradise
Their home when Jesus shall appear.

O precious Faith ! how oft we're taught
What miracles by thee are wrought,
What mountains moved, what battles won,
What foes subdued, what great things done,
What fears allayed, hopes realised,
Earth's vain things scorned, God's good things
    prized !
Such are Faith's works. How great they be !
And what is Faith ?
    Faith, Saviour, is but trust in Thee !

THE SABBATH.

"If thou turn away thy foot from the sabbath, from doing thy pleasure on My holy day; and call the sabbath a delight, the holy of the Lord, honourable; and shalt honour Him, not doing thine own ways, nor finding thine own pleasure, nor speaking thine own words: then shalt thou delight thyself in the Lord; and I will cause thee to ride upon the high places of the earth, and feed thee with the heritage of Jacob thy father."—Isa. lviii. 13, 14.

OUR Saviour has said that the Sabbath was made
    For man—a boon by the Father given,
That the way-worn pilgrim here on earth
    Might taste of the joys of the saints in heaven.

We oftentimes speak of the peaceful rest
    In the home of these glorified saints above;
And we hope to be gathered there at last,
    With all whom we here so fondly love.

We know that there's nothing can compare
    With the bliss of that holy and happy abode;
And the highest wish that our hearts can frame
For ourselves or for them, is that all may claim
    To be welcomed there by our Saviour God.

Now, what are our Sabbaths here below
    But foretastes and shadows of that above?
And could we but always regard them so,
    How dear and how bright would these Sabbaths prove!

But how often we count them a weariness!
    And cry, When will this Sabbath day be done,
That we may betake us again to the race
    For worldly gain? Alas! were it won,

'Twould be at the cost of our precious souls,
    And the loss of all that His love has bought,
Of earthly good or unending bliss,
    For those whom He saved, though they knew Him not

'Till He came—it may be on a Sabbath morn—
    And with healing eyesalve touched their eyes,
And showed them that earth's but a wilderness,—
    The soul's true home is beyond the skies.

Then our earnest aim and effort should be,
If we wish to enjoy Sabbath blessings below,
To bring down to this earth as much of heaven,
Its work and its joys as to saints are given,
Who now, as before in the land of the living,
Are keeping their Sabbath there, Lord, with Thee.

For as Thou art the light of that heaven above,
    So art Thou the fount of all blessing below;
And our Sabbaths here must be spent with Thee,
    If a true Sabbath blessing our hearts would know.

BEULAH.

"A land which the Lord thy God careth for: the eyes of the Lord thy God are always upon it, from the beginning of the year even unto the end of the year."—DEUT. xi. 12.

"All nations shall call you blessed: for ye shall be a delightsome land, saith the Lord of hosts."—MAL. iii. 12.

BEULAH! Beulah! oh, so fair!
    How bless'd are all the dwellers there!
Its genial clime, cerulean skies,
Soft breezes borne from Paradise;
Its hills, with smiling vales between,
With pasture clad so rich and green;
Its mountain peaks which pierce the sky,
Their sides by radiance from on high
Made bright with glory not their own,
But His whose beams are o'er them thrown.
The rills which from these mountains flow
In gay cascades as down they go,

Till, meeting in the plain below,
They form those streams so deep and wide,
Enriching all on every side.
The stately trees of varied hue,
By Spring and Autumn decked anew;
In noble phalanx, broad and grand,
Are gathered some; while others stand
Apart and lone, or scattered o'er
The wide expanse; some skirt the shore
Of rolling stream or lonely lake;
Their quivering leaves the zephyrs shake,
And join with rippling brook to make,
With bleating lambs and lowing herds,
And happy singing of the birds,
Sweet music to delight the ear,
That it with wondering eye may share
The joy abounding everywhere.
While flowers are thrown with lavish hand
Broadcast in beauty o'er the land,
With sweet perfume to scent the air;
And luscious fruit, so rich and rare,
As if our God would nothing spare,
But scatter all with bounteous hand,
To make this a delightsome land.

Yet these are but the shadows, Lord,
Of what Thy goodness doth afford
To those who, guided by Thy hand,
Rest for a while in Beulah Land.
What's best and fairest here below,
Speak of the bliss to which we go,
But, oh, how faintly they express
The fulness of that blessedness!
The sinner saved, God reconciled,
The rebel welcomed as a child,
The filthy cleansed, the naked clothed,
The law fulfilled, sin's service loathed.
For swinish husks—now heavenly bread,
A loving trust for slavish dread,
A certain hope for doubts and fears,
A placid joy for griefs and tears;
Life worthy of the name we bear,
And a patient watch till He appear!

O Covenant! secure and grand!
Like mountain range that fills the land,
A sure retreat no human hand
Could rear, but raised at God's command.
Down from thee flow in rills and streams
Blessings so great, so rich, so free,

Such as faith in her fondest dreams
Could neither ask nor hope to see.
These granted, as seems best to Him,
In trickling rills or copious stream,
By constant flow that cannot tire,
With love our grateful hearts inspire.
His precious promises are made
The hills from which we look for aid;
And in the pages of His word
We find the pastures of our Lord;
There, richly fed, the bruised reed
Becomes a plant of God indeed,
Expanding still, aye towards the sky,
As trees they lift their heads on high,
Firm rooted in the ground they stand—
Jehovah's host—a noble band.
From storm and wind they fear no shock;
For, resting on the living Rock,
Which stable is and stands for aye,
As stable and secure are they.

 Grace helps in every time of need,
  It strengthens, shields, and beautifies,
 Faith's source and stay, and Glory's seed,
  Fits and prepares for Paradise.

THE GOSPEL FEAST.

"A certain man made a great supper, and bade many: ... and said to his servant, Go out quickly into the streets and lanes of the city, ... into the highways and hedges, and compel them to come in, that my house may be filled."—LUKE xiv. 16, 21, 23.

OH, have you not heard of the great feast prepared?
And now open to all who so poorly have fared,
And who never as yet in God's good things have shared,
For they never have heard of this great feast prepared.

'Tis the great marriage feast of the Bridegroom and Bride,
And the Bridegroom is He whom our sins crucified,

While the Bride is the sinners for whom He hath died.
'Tis the great marriage feast of the Bridegroom and Bride.

The espousal was made amid suffering and pain,
But the sufferings are past; peace and joy come again;
And the peace will abide and the joy will remain,
Though th' espousal was made amid suffering and pain.

And 'tis meet when the Bridegroom brings home his fair Bride
In His glory to share, in His palace abide,
Should be mirth and rejoicing on every side;
This is meet when the Bridegroom brings home his fair Bride.

So He sends out His messengers here to proclaim,
And to tell of this feast and invite in His name
Every hungering one. Oh, how gladly they came,
Those messengers sent this great feast to proclaim!

For they go to the east, and they go to the west,
To the north and the south carrying out His behest;
And this upon all was the message they pressed,
In the north and the south, in the east and the west—

" You are hurrying on in a dangerous way,
Oh, stop but a moment and hear us, we pray;
For of weighty import are the words we would say,
While you're hurrying on in this dangerous way.

" You are feeding on husks the swine tread under feet;
You are taking the bitter and calling it sweet;
And instead of God's manna, 'tis ashes you eat,
While you feed on the husks the swine tread under feet.

" And the table above there groans under the load
Of the bountiful banquet, prepared by our God;
Both apples to comfort, and flagons to stay,
And the longing soul satiate in every way
With the bountiful banquet prepared by our God;
On that table above which groans under the load.

"And there's room for us all at this great marriage feast,
And enough for us all of this fare of the best,
And the Bridegroom is there to welcome each guest,
And there's room for us all at this great marriage feast."

So these messengers tell this to all whom they meet,
In the green country lane, or the hard city street,
And each one and all they most lovingly greet;
And in season and out, never cease to entreat
For a loving response to this message so sweet,
While they tell of this great feast to all whom they meet.

Then we'll seek to fill up every yet unfilled chair,
For not one of the seats should be left vacant there;
And no effort we'll grudge and no labour will spare,
While we seek to fill up every yet unfilled chair.

A PRAYER.

"My soul melteth for heaviness: strengthen Thou me according unto Thy word. . . . I will run the way of Thy commandments, when Thou shalt enlarge my heart."—
PSALM cxix. 28, 32.

TAKE me, Father! take and use me,
   Let me something do for Thee!
Long ago Thy grace did choose me,
   But how useless still I be!

Others working all around me,
   Put my indolence to shame;
Can it be that since I found Thee
   I have been Thine but in name?

Oh, forgive my barren greenness,
    Quicken me, O Lord, anew,
Make me fruitful, heal my leanness,
    Show me what Thou'dst have me do.

Make me willing, make me able,
    Strength and will both come from Thee;
For without Thee, I am feeble,
Sinful, worthless, and unstable,
    So but fruitless still must be.

I would look away from self, then,
    Turn me now to Thee alone;
Raise me, Lord, support and strengthen,
Ere the coming shadows lengthen,
    Let Thy will in me be done!

"DID NOT I SEE THEE IN THE GARDEN WITH HIM?"

"Rejoice not over me, O mine enemy: when I fall, I shall arise; when I sit in darkness, the Lord shall be a light unto me."—MICAH vii. 8.

"The Lord upholdeth all that fall, and raiseth up all those that be bowed down."—Ps. cxlv. 14.

So spake the scowling soldier, as he stood
And glared with hatred in its blackest mood,
Alike on Him already in their power,
And the poor trembling wretch, who fain would cower
And shrink from notice in the High Priest's hall,
Though once the foremost, boldest of them all.
So spake the soldier, glorying in the thought
Of one more victim to the slaughter brought,
Forgetful all of what he heard Him say,—
"If Me ye seek, let these then go their way."

So spake poor human nature, in the breast
Of one who tried, now fails to stand the test,
And sadly feels, without His power t' uphold,
The veriest coward indeed, though once in word
    so bold.
His conscience speaks the accusation true,
His faith deserts him, and his boldness too;
He shrinks from suffering, and by sin he tries
To escape the cross, nor cares to win the prize,
Forgetful he of what his Lord did say—
"Fear not, thy faith won't fail; for I for thee will
    pray."

So spake the Saviour, though in bonds He stood
'Mid raging foes all thirsting for His blood;
The fainting servant saw his Master's look—
More full of grace and pity than rebuke,
And louder far than any words it spoke—
"Yes, Peter, in that garden thou with Me
And other loved ones oft wert wont to be.
How blessed there the sweet converse we had,
Without might sorrow be, there we were glad;
And what I then did say I ne'er forget,
I loved Mine own then, and I love them yet."

So SPAKE THE TRUE DISCIPLE, now restored,
Self all abased, and glorying in his Lord—
" Hear me, ye sinners who the Lord have slain,
He died to save you, and He lives again ;
You knew Him not, though David's royal Son,
The promised Saviour.   All His work now done,
To you He sends me and His chosen few,
To tell the wonders of His love to you.
In no one else can saving grace be found,
Come and be saved."

       His fearless words astound,
His boldness awed them, until memory woke,
And told them he who now so fearless spoke
Had companied with Jesus, now adored
As Prince and Saviour ; whom their fathers' God
Had sent to bless and turn them from their sin,
And open His heaven above for them to enter in.

So LET US ALSO SPEAK, when urged to stray
And leave, perchance, the safe though narrow way.
We in the garden oft with Him have been,
And there His suffering and His sorrow seen.
Like Peter, oft we've vowed ne'er to forsake,
And oft like him, alas ! while He did wake,

Who bore such untold sufferings for our sake,
We've slept; and when His enemies appeared
Have turned our backs upon Him, and have feared
Then to be known as His. O gracious Lord,
Help us with that same strength Thou did'st afford
To Peter in his dark and dismal day;
Give us that look which drove despair away;
Help us, like him, Lord, evermore to say—
"All things on earth below or heaven above
Thou knowest, and Thou know'st that Thee we love!"

PERFECT GOD AND PERFECT MAN.

"The man Christ Jesus."—1 TIM. ii. 5.

"Who, being in the form of God, thought it not robbery to be equal with God: but made Himself of no reputation, . . . and was made in the likeness of men."—PHIL. ii. 6, 7.

IN lowly guise the Saviour came,
    A humble virgin's sinless Son;
Assumed an infant's feeble frame,
    Its weakness shared as we have done.

Like us He grew, the child, the lad,
    Submissive to his parents' rule;
A craftsman's home was all he had,
    And trained in honest labour's school,

The Saviour grew from child to man;
    Nor ever left His humble sphere

Till came the hour, when, in God's plan,
    The great Messiah should appear.

Then, like those chosen ones of old,
    Whom God, in dark and cloudy days
From humble sphere in field or fold
    To Israel's help was wont to raise,—
        The Saviour came;
        Oh, praise His name!
Yea, give Him everlasting praise!

But not to Herod's court came He,
    Nor sought His friends in High Priest's hall;
Rude fishermen of Galilee,
    Poor and unlearned, obeyed His call.

And not to deeds of high emprise,
As men would count, did He ordain
To lead them; not to earthly fame,
For victories won on battle plain;
Or loud applause for tuneful strain;
Or eloquence to captivate,
And gain repute in Church or State;
Oh, not to such did He give heed,
Yet His were victories indeed!

They were the meek and lowly few,
  To whom He heavenly truths revealed,
And glorious mysteries brought to view,
  From scribes and Pharisees concealed.

They gathered round Him as He went
  A homeless wanderer to and fro ;
But aye on deeds of mercy bent,
  Moved at the sight of human woe.

They heard His words, they saw His deeds,
  And in their bless'd converse with Him,
A better school by far they found
  Than synagogue or Sanhedrim.

He told them of the Father's love,
  The work which He had come to do,
The Holy Spirit's promised aid,
  And all that He would lead them through.

They wondered at the gracious words
  That from His lips so freely flowed ;
And in them and His miracles
  They recognised the SON OF GOD.

DEATH ENCOUNTERED.

"Forasmuch then as the children are partakers of flesh and blood, He also Himself likewise took part of the same; that through death He might destroy him that had the power of death, that is, the devil; and deliver them who through fear of death were all their lifetime subject to bondage."—HEB. ii. 14, 15.

THERE comes an hour—it comes to all—
    Sad sequel to that fatal fall,
When Adam's sin involved his race
In all its ruin and disgrace;
When life was lost, and death began
To assert its sway o'er sinful man;
And conscious of sin's grievous load,
Man sought to hide himself from God.
That hour must come, must come to all;
For all have sinned—all share the fall.

The spirit which our Father gave
To animate our mortal frame,
And higher good than earthly crave,
Returns to Him from whom it came;
The worn-out body back to dust
Returns from which 'twas ta'en at first.

Death comes, indeed, to all alike,
Yet comes he not alike to all.
Some dread the blow he comes to strike,
Some hear it as the Father's call
To wearied pilgrims as they roam,
Faint, lone, and heart-sick for their home.
They hear it as the Bridegroom's voice,
And when they hear it, they rejoice.

What is it in that dreaded hour
That gives this messenger the power
To shake with fear and terrify?
And oft evokes the sad, vain cry,
"I must not, will not, cannot die!"—
'Tis sin. The conscience, now awake,
Recalls the past and all its deeds—
A black record that well may shake
The trembling frame of him who reads;

And sees by sad experience taught,
God's law despised and set at naught;
The evil heart, the bitter root,
And springing from it as its fruit,
Commandments trampled under foot;
Of all required, not one thing done,
Of all forbade, avoided none:
And love as well as law despised,
God's grace refused, His Christ not prized;
This world, the god that had his heart,
Can now no help nor cheer impart.
O world, how false and vain thou art!

What is it in that solemn hour
Takes from this messenger the power
To terrify? and for distress,
Gives hope and joy and perfect peace;
As if the very calm of heaven,
To dying saints already given,
Enwrapped them in its ample fold;
And crowns, and harps, and streets of gold,
And angels bright; and friends of old
Deemed lost on earth, but now restored;
And blessed presence of their Lord,

Were not unseen, but all enjoyed,
All perfect now and unalloyed.

'Tis faith—faith on the simple word
Of an all-truthful, holy God,
Of Him who will not, cannot lie,
Whose word shall stand and be fulfilled,
Whate'er it be that word shall yield;
Or promised life, or threatened death,
Or richest grace, or fiercest wrath;
That word abides eternally,
The word of Him who cannot lie.

And what, then, in that solemn hour
Does faith reveal, which seems to pour
Such comforts on the dying one?
It tells of the salvation won,
And freely given through God's Son.
Faith does not seek to hide the sin,
But shows the sinner what he's been;
A black record—but still the sight
Brings not despair, but brings to light
More of the glory of that grace,
Which meets and answers such a case—

More of the love of Christ makes known,
More of our need of Christ alone.
It recks not then what we have been,
How deep into God's mysteries seen,
How useful to the Master's cause,
How strictly honoured all His laws,
What converse with Himself have had,
How many souls through us made glad,
What sacrifice we strove to make,
What suffered for the Saviour's sake;
Of none of these the saint doth think
When trembling on the very brink,
And soon into death's arms to sink.
No, none of these are in his thought,
When thus to face life's close he's brought,
His Saviour and his sins are all
Conscience and memory now recall!

No more with questions deep perplexed,
Which often in the past have vexed,
Concerning this world or the next;
He leans now on some simple text,
Which comfort brings alike to sage,
Deep learned in all the sacred page,

Or humble and unlearned one,
Who only knows what Christ has done;
Both rest them on the same sweet word,
Both simply trust the same loved Lord;
They have no other trust beside,
But this—hear it ye sinners far and wide!—
For us Christ Jesus lived, and bled, and died—
His work on earth complete, to heaven He hied,
AND NOW IN HIM ARE ALL HIS PEOPLE'S WANTS SUPPLIED.

DISCIPLESHIP.

"Then said Jesus to those . . . which believed on Him, If ye continue in My word, then are ye My disciples indeed."—JOHN viii. 31.

"Herein is My Father glorified, that ye bear much fruit; so shall ye be My disciples."—JOHN xv. 8.

LORD Jesus! may I take the name,
    And really Thy disciple be?
Thou may'st, indeed, for unto all
    My call is, Come and learn of Me.

Lord Jesus! should I take the name,
    And really Thy disciple be?
Thou should'st—thou'rt lost unless thou dost—
    Salvation's only found in Me.

Lord Jesus! can I take the name,
    And really Thy disciple be?
Without My aid, My Spirit says,
    No man can ever come to Me.

Poor sinner! wilt thou take the name,
    And truly My disciple be?
Thou may'st, thou should'st, thou can'st, for free
    The Spirit is for all—for thee.

Poor sinner! if thou only wilt,
    There's nothing that can hinder thee;
The Father loves, My blood is spilt,
    The Spirit waits thy help to be.

Lord Jesus! I would take the name,
    And truly Thy disciple be;
I feel the Father draws; I pray,
    O Holy Spirit, strengthen me.

Poor sinner! come and take the name,
    And truly My disciple be.

This now you know—I tell you so—
All My disciples have to do,
   Is hear, and trust, and follow Me.

Lord Jesus! I will take the name,
   And truly Thy disciple be;
I'm poor, and weak, unwise, and wrong;
But Thou art rich, and wise, and strong;
And all that may to Thee belong
   Is mine,—so I have all in Thee!

THE EVER-LIVING SAVIOUR.

These verses have already been published and circulated as a leaflet.

"I am He that liveth, and was dead; and, behold, I am alive for evermore, Amen; and have the keys of hell and of death."—REV. i. 18.

The writer of the following lines makes no claim to originality in either their thought or expression. They are but the outburst of, he trusts, a thankful heart, written after a pleasant Sabbath spent in waiting upon God in the ordinary services of the Sanctuary; and they are now presented to the public in the hope that they may touch a responsive chord in the hearts of others who may be rejoicing, like him, in Christ Jesus as their ever-living Saviour.

COME! let us sing to Christ our King
    A joyous song of praise,
And in our hearts make melody,
    While we our voices raise.
For Jesus lived and Jesus died,
    And Jesus lives again;
And Jesus stands at God's right hand,
    His kingdom to maintain.

Our fathers, in their rites and types,
    Afar off saw His day;
And faith in Him who was to come
    Was all their hope and stay.
But better days on us have dawned,
    We see the Saviour come;
And FAITH, and HOPE, and LOVE, and JOY,
    Now cheer our pilgrim home.

Our FAITH beholds the Lamb of God
    Atone for all our sin;
And HOPE looks up, and sees the bliss
    His righteousness doth win.
And LOVE to Him pervades our souls
    Who loved us while we strayed,
Who sent His Son to save the lost,
    And bring the helpless aid.

And LOVE to Him, who gladly came
    To do the Father's will;
Who takes our place and bears our sin,
    And answers for us still.
And LOVE to Him whose touch awakes,
    And all this grace reveals;

Who brings us to our Saviour's feet,
    And every promise seals.

And LOVE to them who fear His name,
    Who tremble at His word;
And, linked in loving brotherhood,
    Adore Him as their Lord.
And LOVE to them who wander still—
    Such as the Master showed—
We hate their sins, but love their souls,
    And woo them back to God.

We tell them Jesus lived and died,
    That Jesus lives again;
And they that trust to Him for all,
    Can never trust in vain.
Then let us sing to Christ our King
    A joyous song of praise,
And in our hearts make melody,
    While we our voices raise.

And, while we sing to Christ our King,
    We'll let our joy be seen!

We're not yet what we hope to be,
    We are not what we've been ;
But by His grace we're moving on,
    And keep the narrow road,
Where, lightened by His countenance,
    We journey home to God.

Earth's storms may beat, her waters rage,
    Nay, hell itself assail ;
But sheltered 'neath His loving wings,
    No foe can e'er prevail.
The weakest lamb within His fold
    Enjoys His constant care ;
And none but those He leads and guides
    Can find an entrance there.

But, once within its hallowed walls,
    Oh, how supremely blessed !
Light to the dark, life to the dead,
    And to the weary rest ;
Sight to the blind, strength to the lame,
    Health to the sick He brings ;
Deaf ears, unstopped, now gladly hear ;
    The tongue once dumb now sings.

Even now He owns us for His sons,
  And, with a Father's care,
Guides and provides for all our wants,
  Feeds us on heavenly fare.
But soon He'll call us to Himself,
  Or will Himself appear;
We'll be with Him where He is now,
  Or He'll be with us here.

Yes! Jesus lived, and Jesus died,
  And Jesus comes again;
He comes again to judge the world,
  He comes again to reign.
To reign, not o'er a little flock,
  Obscure, despised, and few;
All heaven and earth shall own His sway,
  And Satan's legions too.

Angels and saints exulting see
  Redemption-work complete,
And he who erewhile bruised His heel
  Lies crushed beneath His feet.
For Jesus lived, and Jesus died,
  And Jesus lives again;

And Jesus sits upon His throne,
　　And shall for ever reign.

Then now we'll sing to Christ our King
　　A joyous song of praise,
And in our hearts make melody,
　　While we our voices raise.
For then our feeble strains will merge
　　In loud acclaims of praise,
Which angel-hosts and ransomed saints
　　In one grand anthem raise!

THE OPENED EYE.

"Open Thou mine eyes, that I may behold wondrous things."—Ps. cxix. 18.

"One thing I know, that, whereas I was blind, now I see."—John ix. 25.

LORD! when I inward turn mine eye,
   What is the sight that then I see?
A heart polluted and unclean,
   At enmity with good and Thee.

Lord! when I backward turn mine eye,
   What is the sight that then I see!
A life of wickedness and sin,
From youth to age continued in,
   Defying or forgetting Thee.

Lord! when I forward turn mine eye,
    What is the sight that then I see?
The Judge upon the great white throne,
The sinner, friendless and undone,
Condemned, not by the Judge alone,
But forced himself his guilt to own,
    And acquiesce in the decree,
    Natheless its endless misery,
Which then, O Lord! pronounced by Thee,
    Tells of a lost Eternity!

Lord! when I upward turn mine eye,
    What is the sight that then I see?
The Father, Son, and Spirit met,
The great Triune in council set,
    The mystery of redemption planned,
    The work committed to His hand,
Who at the appointed season came,
And, ever blessèd be His name,
Endured the cross, despised the shame,
That through Him sinners now might claim
    Acceptance with the holy God,—
    Pardon for all the ill they've done,—
    Deliverance from its galling load,—
And likeness to the righteous One.

So when I forward turn mine eye,
    This is the sight that now I see—
Through life a pardoned sinner led,
    In all his way kept, Lord, by Thee;
And when the Judgment-seat is set,
    Stands at the bar, but not alone—
Still owns indeed his deepest guilt,
But knows the blood for him once spilt
    Was that of Him now on the throne,
    Who bought and claims him for His own,—
He hears with joy the glad decree,
Which then, O Lord! pronounced by Thee,
    Tells of a bless'd Eternity!

WILLING TO DEPART.

"We are . . . willing rather to be absent from the body, and to be present with the Lord."—2 COR. v. 8.

"With Christ; which is far better."—PHIL. i. 23.

THE glorious "Whosoever will;"
    The sure "I'll in no wise cast out;"
The "blood that cleanseth from all sin;"
    The gracious "Wherefore did ye doubt?"

These, and a thousand texts like these,
    Dispel all doubts and cheer the heart;
They fill the soul with perfect peace,
    And make us willing to depart.

And then the sight He sometimes gives
    Of what the saints enjoy above;

Bright visions of His own bless'd face,
    And gushings of His heart of love!

When thus He deals with suffering ones,
    On beds of sickness though they lie,
His presence for their pain atones,
    And makes them even glad to die.

It may be sad from friends to part,
    And leave those whom we dearly love;
But for us all He has prepared
    A better home by far above.

There, in a little while, we know
    His ransomed ones shall gathered be;
All sickness, pain, and partings o'er,
    And all rejoicing, Lord, in Thee!

All that Thy life and death secure,
    To all who trust Thee freely given,
Pardon, and Peace, and Righteousness,
    And everlasting bliss in heaven!

OLD BETTY.

"Have not I written to thee excellent things, . . . that I might make thee know the certainty of the words of truth?"
—Prov. xxii. 20, 21.

"The Comforter, which is the Holy Ghost, whom the Father will send in My name, He shall teach you all things."
—John xiv. 26.

OLD Betty was born 'mong our Highland hills,
    Long before such things as Board Schools
       were known;
So, while she was strong both in body and limb,
And grew up a lassie well-favoured and trim,
Of book-lore, alas! the poor body got none.

In the days of her youth, too, the reaping machines
Had not been invented to cut down the grain;

But trooping in crowds, burly loons and stout queans
Came down from our Highland hills, down to the plain
As each harvest came round; and our farmers were glad,
When they looked on their fields so abundantly clad,
To see such an army with sickle and plaid,
Appear in their time of need, bringing them aid.

So year after year did Betty come down,
And it turned out at last with a favourite loon,
Who found favour not only in her loving eyes
But in those of the farmer they served, who thought wise
The permanent service of both to retain,
Instead of but helping to cut down his grain.

They left then their Highland home up in the hills;
And while he, as farmer's man, followed the plough,
She wrought, as she said, "among a' orra things
Round the steading connected with cattle or cow."
And so the years passed in industry and quiet,
And few were the changes that fell to their lot.

They lived without God—alas! how many try it
They lived on His care, but remember'd Him not.

But there came a day when He thought upon them,
And to keep them from settling down in their nest,—
It might be a rude waking, but surely to Him
Who does everything well, we must own it was best;
The husband was stricken at last by disease,
And he lay and groaned under his sufferings sore,
But the pain that he felt in his poor mortal frame
Was but light as compared with that which now
    came
To pierce his sad soul; and it vexed him far more
To think that when now he looked death in the
    face
He should not be ready, but all unprepared;
For he never had learned of the matchless grace
Of the God to whom he had given no place
In all his thoughts; and now that the race
Was so nearly run, he scarcely dared
To utter a prayer, but vacantly stared
Into coming gloom, as if no one cared
For his perishing soul, and thus he lay
As one condemned while passing away.

No olive plants round their table had sprung,
They grew old together a childless pair;
Yet the music of childish prattle rung
Through their cottage home, for a child was there.
A child, alas! of sin and of shame,
Whom heartless parents refused to own,
And handed o'er to a stranger's care,
And suffered to borrow a stranger's name,
That she might never by theirs be known.

This little one, now but a child of seven,
Had been sent by them to the village school,
And had learned sweet hymns about God and heaven,
Which, tho' hid from their darkened minds, were full
Of precious truths, even truths that could save;
For they spake of Christ's cradle, His cross, and His grave.
She had got, too, as a reward at school,
A little book which she highly prized,—
'Twas a copy, indeed, of God's own Word,
So precious for all, yet so often despised,—
Its pages she conned o'er and o'er again,
And spelt out the words oft with trouble and pain,

And those which were long and beyond her power,
The poor little one had just to pass o'er.
She was reading the gospel of John one day,
While the poor dying man in his suffering lay;
And he hearkened and heard, as he lay on his bed,
And this was the verse, and thus it was read—

"GOD SO LOVED THE WORLD, THAT HE GAVE HIS ONLY —— SON, THAT —— —— IN HIM SHOULD NOT PERISH, BUT HAVE —— LIFE."

Thus he heard of God's love, he heard of God's
    Son,
He heard of God's gift, and of life begun,—
But these gaps were left, and he could not yet see
For whom, and in what way, these great things
    could be;
Yet he felt that these truths quite suited his case,
And he cried to his wife, "If any pass by,
Bring in the first one, and ask him to try
To read the whole verse, and explain it to us."
A lad was brought in, and he reads the verse
    thus—

"GOD SO LOVED THE WORLD, THAT HE GAVE HIS ONLY BEGOTTEN SON, THAT WHOSOEVER BELIEVETH IN HIM SHOULD NOT PERISH, BUT HAVE EVERLASTING LIFE."

He heard, and he cried, "Oh! I know what's believ-
    ing,
It's nothing but trust; and I know everlasting,
But what's whosoever? oh! that I can't see."
Says the lad, "It is any one—just you or me."
"Just any one, say you? I see now, I see!
I thank Thee, O God, for this goodness to me,
And now I can die, only trusting in Thee!"

The Spirit was there, and He wrought not in vain,
For another poor sinner was then born again.

Oh, who can depict the joy that then beamed
On the face of that dying man? Surely it seemed
As if Jesus Himself again had appeared,
And thrown down the bulwark that Satan had reared
'Tween Him and this ransomed one, given of God
A fresh witness to be to the power of His blood.

Oh, blessèd the moment when light rushes in,
And the Spirit applies God's ransom for sin,
When the darkness is gone, and the sinner now sees
Not only his sins, but God's refuge from these.

He lingered on still for a week or two more,
And daily he fed on fresh truth freely given;
And at last closed his eyes in peace here on earth,
To be opened again in the full bliss of heaven!

Poor Betty was left now alone with the child
To bring up and to share in her desolate lot;
But the blessing of God and His own blessed light
Were shed down and abode on her poor lowly cot.
'Twas the Spirit that taught the poor dying one,
And He was still present with them that were left,
And a sev'nfold care seemed to lavish on them,
Of their earthly support and their stay now bereft.

There is no one, indeed, that teaches like Him;
And pleasing the tale that I now have to tell,
How poor Betty, who'd never been taught in her youth,
In her riper years learned to read, and read well.

'Twas the dear little child by whom she was taught,
And the Bible the book they both eagerly scanned ;
And the truth, as they read with slow progress but
    sure,
Took all the more hold, for they could not endure
To pass over a verse and not understand
Its full meaning; and so, not the letter alone,
But the truth in its spirit and power came home
To hearts all prepared to receive the good seed,
And produce not mere hearers, but doers indeed.

'Twas the work of the Spirit, whose office it is
To take of God's truths and reveal them to His.
Who may be but babes in His kingdom, and poor,
But unto whom still is His promise made sure—
That the meek and the lowly ones ever shall find
What is hid from the proud and self-satisfied mind.

So they aye read their Bible, and oft through and
    through ;
To either of them 'twas the One Book they knew,
And they spake of its truths in such wondrous wise,
It filled all their neighbours around with surprise ;
For Betty now knows her dear Bible so well,
She is counted a "mother in Israel!"

RESTORED.

"He restoreth my soul."—Ps. xxiii. 3.

"I will restore health unto thee, and I will heal thee of thy wounds, saith the Lord."—Jer. xxx. 17.

O SINNER! caught in Satan's snare,
    Led to deny your Lord!
Sink not and yield not to despair,
    You yet may be restored.

Oh, think not lightly of your sin!
    It deeply wounds His heart;
But still that Heart yearns over you,
    Unwilling to depart—

And leave you in the tempter's power,
    To glory in your fall,
And lead you back to bondage dire,
    And sin's unending thrall.

Write bitter things against yourself,
    And tears of sorrow shed,
You never can bewail enough
    The sins for which He bled.

But add not sinful unbelief
    To sin you now deplore;
Mistrusting both His word and grace
    But makes your guilt the more.

Like Peter, look to Jesus' face,
    And see the love that's there;
In the sad look you give to Him
    He'll recognise a prayer—

A prayer, though not expressed in words,
    Well understood by Him;
Thine answer to His look of love
    That stirs thy heart within.

What can you do with sin but go
    To the still open door,
And wash anew in Jesus' blood
    As you have done before?

There only, peace and pardon found
    Shall nerve your heart anew,
And strengthened faith will strengthen love,
    And inward sin subdue.

'Tis only keeping near to Him
    And trusting Him with all,
You'll run the race successfully,
    And keep from future fall.

SALVATION'S STORY.

"So great salvation."—Heb. ii. 3.
"Salvation is of the Lord."—Jonah ii. 9.
"The Lord is my strength and song, and is become my salvation."—Ps. cxviii. 14.

COME, let us think of Jesus,
    Of Jesus and His love;
Who came from heaven to save us,
    Leaving His throne above,

And the bosom of the Father,
    For He was His delight;
And the praises of the angels
    Unceasing day and night;

In that bright home so holy,
    Without a taint of sin,
And where no pain nor sorrow
    Can ever enter in.

Oh, its blessedness was perfect!
    God reigning over all;
And a cheerful service rendered
    To Him by great and small;

A willing, true obedience,
    And submission to His will,
Ensured this perfect blessedness—
    A bliss abiding still.

But another fold He thought of;
    And it grieved God at His heart
That the foe this fold had entered,
    And seduced man to depart

From Him and from His service,
    Such as angels give above,
That as angels they might share in
    His blessings and His love.

But they listened to the tempter,
    And, deceivèd by his lies,
Rebelled against their Maker,
    And learned, with opened eyes,

That the way of the transgressor,
    Which henceforth they would tread,
Was hard and full of bitterness
    And death, as God had said.

And so, in sad forgetfulness
    Of Jehovah and His ways,
In fearful sin and misery
    They passed their wretched days.

For Satan triumphed over them,
    And held them in his power:
And sin and death reigned rampant
    As the unhappy dower

Which forsaking God had brought them,
    When they disbelieved His Word,
And put more faith in Satan
    Than their Creator-Lord.

But though they had forsaken Him,
    He still remembered them;
And His thoughts were still of mercy full,
    All unwilling to condemn,

Or to leave them in their misery.
    So the Father sent the Son
To be their Saviour, by atoning
    For the sin that they had done.

The Messiah came most gladly
    To do all the Father's will;
And lived and died for sinners,
    And answers for them still.

He took our nature on Him,
    Became a little Child:
Though God, as Man He suffered,
    But ne'er by sin defiled.

Himself a spotless sacrifice,
    He on the altar bled:
God's justice thus was satisfied
    By His dying in our stead.

And His life of spotless innocence
    And freedom from all sin,
Provides us with a righteousness
    Through which we enter in

Again into God's favour,
    As sinners reconciled;
And no longer guilty rebels,
    He counts each one a child,

When, all other trust renouncing,
    We build our hope on Him,
Who came to earth from heaven
    This lost world to redeem.

Oh, then, I'll think of Jesus,
    And all He's done for me;
And when temptation rises,
    To His dear arms I'll flee.

When Satan would assail me,
    I'll tell him Jesus died;
So he no more can claim me,
    For I am justified

By the work my Saviour finished,
    When He died upon the tree;
Since for all my Master answers,
    He can nothing find in me.

I'll refer him to that Master,
    Who will ever shelter me —
And tell Satan from his bondage
    I've been by Him set free.

And I'll trust my all to Jesus;
    And from His fulness still,
I'll aye draw all that's needed
    To conform me to God's will.

For, though He's gone to heaven,
    He leaves me not alone:
The Holy Ghost, the Comforter,
    Whom He promised to His own;

Hath come, and will uphold me,
    Console me and instruct,
And, in the path assigned me,
    Aye safely me conduct.

He'll apply the work of Jesus
    To my sin-burdened soul;
For Father, Son, and Spirit
    All combine to make me whole.

My Lord will ne'er forsake me:
    But, protected by His power,
He will keep me safe, and make me
    All ready for that hour,

When His will shall be to take me
    To see Him in His glory,
As the blessed consummation
    Of His salvation's story.

"DO YOU LOVE GOD?"

"God hath chosen the weak things of the world to confound the things which are mighty."—1 COR. i. 27.

"A little child shall lead them."—ISA. xi. 6.

"Do you love God?" 'Twas a childish voice
   That spoke thus in accents so soft and so mild;
But the Spirit-sent arrow flew straight to its place,
   Though the bow that was drawn was drawn by a child.

Returning now home from her bright holidays,
   She happened to meet, in the home-going train,

With a kind-hearted one, whom her sweet, winning
    ways
  Had so charmed and amused, that again and again
Did he ply the dear maiden with story and fun,
To beguile the long road as the moments ran on.

So he joked, and she laughed and screamed with
    delight,
  And the dearest of friends all at once they be-
    came,
Till, in talk with another, he mentioned God's
    name—
  Without reverence, I fear—indeed, took it in vain;
  Yet, strange as it seems, without giving her pain.

For she had been always accustomed to hear
  That Name ever spoken with love and with awe,
So made sure her new friend was a friend of God
    too;
  And when she thus questioned, she thought she
    might draw
Some sweet declaration of love to the God
  Who so early had found her, and in whose dear
    love

She had found such delight, and whose favour she
    prized,
  Than her nearest and dearest all others above.

He turned to the little one, patted her head,
  And sought to put off his reply with a smile;
But the questioning look on her face still remained,
  And would not give way. So, after a while—
" Love God, my sweet darling? Pray, tell me, do
    you?"
  Was the answer he made. "To be sure, Sir, I
    do;
And all who love me, I know, do love Him too.
  Now, you've been very kind, and I see you love
    me;
So I'm wanting to know from you how this may
    be,
  And this is the reason I'm questioning thee."

The arrow struck home, and would not be removed,
  And it led him to think of his earlier days—
Of a father revered and a mother beloved,
  Training him to love God, and delight in His
    ways.

He thought how he'd wandered, forgotten this God,
    Neglected His service, and broken His laws;
He saw himself vile and exposed to God's wrath,
    And he trembled while feeling how helpless he was.

But he thought of the lessons he'd learned in his youth,
    Of the love of this God to our poor fallen race;
And found comfort at last in embracing the truth,
    As revealed in that wondrous old story of grace.

Thus the Spirit made use of the little child's words,
    A fresh trophy to bring to the power of this grace,
And to show that from babes' and from suckling mouths
    He can still, when it pleases Him, perfect His praise.

IN MEMORIAM.

The following lines have already appeared in the author's little book "ONLY A SERVANT." The first nine stanzas were written by the brother of Mary H——, the subject of that memoir, as a tribute of affection to the memory of his sister. The succeeding verses were added by the writer of the memoir:—

IN the bright and blooming summer,
    When the fields were green,
We have mused on varied beauties,
    Where we oft have been.
But the winter came, my sister,
    Like a night of pall,
Dropping dews of death upon thee,
    Dearest flower of all.

Oh, my sister, sad and lonely
    I am left to mourn ;

Never shall thine arms entwine me,
    Evermore forlorn !
But thine eye will beam upon me
    From the realm above,
As I seek to learn the mission
    Of a Saviour's love.

There was none on earth to guide us
    In the days of youth,
None to point a nobler pathway
    To the realms of truth ;
Each parental voice was silent
    In the grave's deep lair,
But within the blessed Eden
    Thou hast met them there.

Passed the hours of joyous childhood,
    Days of flower and fern,
Opening upon a world
    That was dark and stern ;
But thy smile was ever gladsome
    As the sunny ray,
Guiding me in hours of danger
    Through the narrow way.

Gentle as the evening zephyr
    Rippling o'er the lea,
Sweet as perfume of the garden
    Thou hast been to me;
And in sacred, solemn moments,
    By thy guiding hand,
Thou hast pointed out the glory
    Of the better land.

With a love that never faltered,
    With a humble mind,
Thou didst seek to soothe the sorrows
    Of our human kind;
Counting they were wasted moments,
    Registered above,
If thou wert not pointing others
    To the Lord of love.

Thou art with me still my sister,
    In the silent night,
When the stars beam in the azure
    With a pensive light;
And I seem to hear thy footstep,
    And thy gentle tone;

But there comes the wakeful morning,
    And I am alone.

With a smile of peace, serenely
    Thou hast passed from earth,
To a bright and happy heaven,
    To the newer birth !
Where all pain is lost in blessing,
    Where all grief is gone,
Sunk amidst the endless glories
    That surround the throne.

We are left behind thee, sister,
    But we can't repine ;
'Twas the will of our Great Father,
    It was also thine ;
And the darkness that was looming,
    Changes now to light,
Where triumphant saints are standing,
    Clothed in robes of white.

There, amidst the happy number,
    Thou hast ta'en thy place,

Added to the heavenly circle,
   By His sovereign grace;
There I hope to meet thee, sister,
   When my time shall come,
Ransomed by the same Redeemer
   Who has called thee home.

Thou didst pray—ay, wrestle for me:
   Yet the cries and tears
Wrung from thee, were answered by me
   But with gibes and sneers:
Now I lay my rebel weapons
   At my Saviour's feet;
Own me vanquished, and betake me
   To the humblest seat.

Learning, with a lowly spirit,
   Like a little child,
And with pride of human wisdom,
   Am no more beguiled!
But as thou believ'dst, believing
   In His written word,
Find, as thou didst find, a faithful,
   Covenant-keeping Lord.

Poor, and blind, and vile, and naked,
    Having nought but sin,
I will flee to Him for refuge,
    He will take me in ;
He'll enrich, and cleanse, and clothe me,
    Oh, how fair the dress !
In the Father's eyes so pleasing !
    His own righteousness !

Lost in Him—no more a sinner,
    But a child of God,
I will follow in the pathway,
    Thou with Him hast trod;
Weak and worthless, needing all things,
    Look to Him on high ;
Daily grace for daily duty,
    Aye will be my cry.

I will live as thou hast taught me,
    Follow in thy wake ;
Hoping, working, bearing, trusting,
    All for Jesus' sake.
And when comes the solemn summons,
    Hear my Saviour's call,

Joyful hear it, as thou heard'st it --
    Nothing to appal.

Nothing in it to discourage;
    Can the Father's voice,
Calling home His loved ones to Him,
    Bid them but rejoice?
There I'll meet thee then, my sister;
    Through the grace of God,
Another guilty sinner ransomed
    By thy Saviour's blood!

Led by thee to look unto Him—
    When we reach the goal,
Thine will be the added lustre
    Of thy brother's soul,
Given to thine earnest pleadings
    At the throne of grace—
Thy most loved among thy many
    Turned to righteousness.

THE GIFTS OF GRACE.

"All that the Father giveth Me shall come to Me; and him that cometh to Me I will in no wise cast out."—JOHN vi. 37.

"Holy Father, keep through Thine own name those whom thou hast given Me. . . . Those that Thou gavest Me I have kept, and none of them is lost."—JOHN xvii. 11, 12.

THE Father gave me to the Son
   From all eternity;
And oh, with what unceasing care
   Has He watched over me!

Like all, into this world of sin,
   I came a fallen man—
God's image marred, by sin debased,
   In Satan's ways I ran.

But even then, how rich the grace
  By which I was restrained,
And led through all the devious paths
  Wherein I'd still remained,

Had not that grace at length appeared,
  In all its mighty power,
Laid hold on me, and struck me down
  In that thrice blessed hour,

When light from Heaven itself arose,
  Than brightness of the sun
More bright. It shone on sinful me,
  And then the work was done.

The work was done; but not by me.
  His was the blessed light
That round me shone, and His the rays
  That gave my spirit sight.

And His the voice that called to me—
  A voice so full of power—
Revealing both myself and Him
  In that same blessed hour—

Myself, in all my guilt and sin,
    At enmity with God;
Himself, in all His grace and love,
    Come to remove that load.

He found me poor—He made me rich;
    Blind—but gave sight to me;
Vile—but He washed me in His blood;
    Bound—but He set me free;

Cold—but He shed abroad His love
    In this hard heart of mine;
Dark—but my ignorance dispelled,
    And taught me truth divine.

He took away the filthy rags
    That could not cover me,
That in His own pure righteousness,
    All comely, I might be.

He found me weak—He gave me strength;
    Of all He had to give
Himself He emptied—gave to me,
    And died that I might live!

O wondrous love ! O grace divine !
   Was e'er so rich a store
Of blessing known?—so full, so free—
   And theirs for evermore

Who will but hearken to His voice,—
   Take what He longs to give:
His message still is, "Come to Me!
   Hear, and your soul shall live!"

No cumbrous rite of sacrifice,
   No vain attempt to DO:
All that was needed He has done,
   And now all's free to you.

THE AGED PILGRIM'S SOLILOQUY.

"Knowing that shortly I must put off this my tabernacle, even as our Lord Jesus Christ hath shewed me."—2 PETER i. 14.

FRIENDS of my youth! Oh, how many are gone!
While I am left lingering here all alone.
Playmates and schoolmates of earliest days—
How soon were we parted and lost in the maze
Of this fleeting world, with its changes and cares—
Uncertain, unstable, and in these long years,
Fond memory fails to recall ev'n the names
Of our once well-known rivals in lessons and games.
Ye are gone! and long since to the righteous award
Have the most of you bowed, of our merciful Lord;
Some leaving behind them the blessed perfume

Of a life of faith, lived by His grace here below,
Their leaving this earth, but a bright going home,
And entering the joy which His ransomed ones know.

And I am left here all alone for a time,
A little while longer life's burden to bear.
Even so, Righteous Father, let Thy will be done.
It contents me.   All's well if Thou only art near.
I've sinned and I've suffered, but by Thee been led
To the foot of the cross, where my dear Saviour
    bled.
I am looking to Jesus—in Him I'm complete–
So, with God-given faith, I'll still cling to His feet,
And all that Thou sendest be ready to meet.

This tottering tent, in which my soul's housed,
Gives tokens as if its cords soon would be loosed ;
And these pains, and these aches, and this failing
    of strength,
Are but whispers to tell me He's coming at length.
It may not be long till His messenger come ;
And this sickness may prove, though I under it
    groan,
But the gate of the pathway by which I'm led home.

RETROSPECTION.

"I have been young, and now am old; yet have I not seen the righteous forsaken."—Ps. xxxvii. 25.

"We spend our years as a tale that is told."—Ps. xc. 9.

"Surely goodness and mercy shall follow me all the days of my life."—Ps. xxiii. 6.

SEVENTY years! Threescore and ten!
The limit that God has assigned to men.
How seldom attained, and when it is done,
And the full tale of the years has been run,
How short, at the close, the whole limit appears,
Even the full tale of the seventy years!

Seventy years! Threescore and ten!
Oh, how I remember, with grief and with shame,

How often I've striven against my God,
And counted His service a grievous load!
Though the brightest hours that ever I spent
Were those which I to that service lent,
And, in hallowed communion with Him and with His,
Had a taste here on earth of His heavenly bliss!

Seventy years! Threescore and ten!
I've companied here with my fellow-men.
But oh, how little, by word or deed
Have I sought to help them in their need.
I have seen them perishing, heard their cry,
But, bound up in selfishness, passed them by.

Seventy years! Threescore and ten!
Spent in a world of suffering and sin.
Oh, what in that time might not I have done
In work for the Master; and, like God's dear Son,
Healed the sick, soothed the dying, and hungry ones fed,
As He did, with both earthly and heavenly bread!

Seventy years! Threescore and ten!
Oh, could I but live it all over again,
How unlike the past my future would be!
I'd live not for time, but eternity!
For time's best things do so speedily pass;
They may please for a while, but they wither like
    grass!

Seventy years! Threescore and ten!
They are past, and will never return again;
But they've left behind them a full record
Of every thought, and deed, and word.
And for all I have spoken and thought and done,
I must answer at last at the Great White Throne!

Seventy years! Threescore and ten!
Will seem less than the twinkling eyelid then.
But oh, the dread import of one little word,
Deed, or thought, when then standing before the
    Lord,
When all must submit to the judgment of God,
And all must then reap of whatever they've
    sowed!

Seventy years! Threescore and ten!
I may wish to live it all over again,
But, wish as I may, I know it is vain;
What is past can ne'er be recalled again.
But there's One that has given His life for me,
And He has been all that I've failed to be.

Seventy years! Threescore and ten!
Not half of that time He lived among men;
But He lived, and loved, and suffered, and bled;
Was buried, but rising again from the dead,
And, alive evermore, to heaven has sped;
And there, as the Lamb that was once crucified,
Pleads for those for whom here He both lived and
    died.

Seventy years! Threescore and ten!
They only live who are born again;
And the life that they lead even here now on earth
They reckon it not from their earthly birth;
But the date of the birthday which now they give
Is when Jesus passed by them and bade them
    live.

Seventy years! Threescore and ten!
There's no such limit to their life then;
It begins here on earth, but continues to run
Through ages eternal. This life's in God's Son;
And as He endures everlastingly,
Even such shall the life of His ransomed ones be.

Seventy years! Threescore and ten!
Should more of my mortal life remain,
Let it all be given, O Lord, to Thee!
For pardon and peace to Thy cross I would flee,
Thy finished work still is my only plea.
Make me whate'er Thou wouldst have me to be;
And when, through death, to life I awake,
Take me home to Thy heaven, for Jesus' sake!

THE FLIGHT OF TIME.

"So teach us to number our days, that we may apply our hearts unto wisdom. . . . O satisfy us early with Thy mercy; that we may rejoice and be glad all our days."—Ps. xc. 12, 14.

HOW quickly do our moments fly,
 Hours speed so rapidly away;
Before we wot, to-day is past,
 To-morrow changed to yesterday!

Weeks seem to end ere well begun,
 And months look shorter than before;
Spring, Summer, Autumn, run their course,
 And Winter's back when barely o'er.

It was not so when life was young;
    We thought in early childhood's days,
"As happy as the day is long,"
    A wise and most expressive phrase.

And ere the youth became a man,
    Or maiden into matron grew,
Hope long deferred and bliss delayed
    Their darksome shadows o'er them threw.

Time seemed to them a laggard then,
    And each day longer than the last;
Weeks, months, and years, a weary tale
    Of tiresome time, would ne'er be past!

But is not time aye still the same?
    Just sixty minutes to the hour
Is what we calculate to-day—
    In days bygone it was no more.

Then, why the change which now we feel?
    As if that time had shorter grown,
And, with accelerated pace,
    Just shows itself, then rushes on.

Ah, is it, say, because when young
    We think we've such a vast supply,
Our lease of time won't soon be run;
    And so we live more leisurely?

And on the web which all must weave
    We ply the shuttle soft and slow,
And bending quietly o'er the loom,
We hurry not, and find there's room
    To watch the patterns as they grow.

But when long years have come and gone,
    We know the end is drawing near;
And shorter threads in life's stern web
    Are sooner interwoven there.

The shorter thread is sooner sped
    Athwart the weary loom;
And lower in the emptying glass
The fewer grains more quickly pass,
    As the sand is running down.
And as the race draws to a close,
"Tis short, quick spurts the runner throws
Into the struggle as he goes;
    And then the goal is won.

GOD IN NATURE AND IN GRACE.

"The Lord is good to all: and His tender mercies are over all His works."—Ps. cxlv. 9.

"How great is His goodness, and how great is His beauty!"—Zech. ix. 17.

OH, there's many a glorious scene on earth,
    Where the stable mountains, calm and grand,
In all their stern beauty, are standing forth
As they came at the first from their Maker's hand.
And it fills our souls with a holy awe,
As on summit or peak entranced we gaze,
Or note with delight how each seeming flaw
In their rugged sides, when the sun's bright rays
Are o'er them thrown, a fresh beauty displays.

And we cry, as we notice the light and the shade,
"Oh, how fair is this world which our God has
    made!"

Or we stand, it may be, by the calm seaside,
And gaze on the ebb or the flow of the tide,
And the gentle ripple and ceaseless flow
Of the tiny waves, as they come and go
On the wide expanse of the glistening sand—
The barrier firm 'tween the sea and the land—
Fills our souls with peace and a quiet rest,
Like a ship becalmed on that ocean's breast.
Or, it may be, when storms and tempests roar,
Again we are found on old Ocean's shore;
And the calm is supplanted now by the grand,
And the boiling waves rush over the land;
And the rampart rocks can scarce withstand
The rush and the roar and the fearful shocks
Of these raging waves on the steadfast rocks;
And the waves dissolve in an angry spray,
As if weeping because they had lost their prey,
And, in failing to drive these rocks away,
With pain and with anger they now confessed
Their baffled attempt to escape their unrest,

By o'erleaping the limits in which they've found,
By a firm decree, they are always bound.
But be it the calm or be it the grand,
The steadfast rocks or the shifting sand,
They both are there at our God's command;
And, gazing on each, we still have said,
"Oh, how fair is this world which our God has
    made!"

Oh, there's many a beautiful spot on earth,
Sweet, quiet nooks in a sunny glade,
With a rippling brook running softly through,
And all on its grassy banks are laid
A rich display, in their varied hue;
But, shining in all their loveliness,
Of these tiny flowerets God has made,
Through them His care of us to express,
And to teach us that none need be afraid
That His loving care of His own could cease.
The rippling brook, and the flowery banks,
And the sunbeams glinting through the trees,
And the air perfumed by the balmy scent
Spread all around by the gentle breeze.
Amid scenes like these how oft we have said,
" How fair is this world which our God has made!"

There is many a happy home on earth
Where love and peace reign ; for God hath designed
The humble rôle of the household hearth
The fittest arena where man can find
Full scope for nurturing every grace,
That in His appointment finds a place
In His plan for the weal of human kind.
And so it is there alone that we find
Such peace and such quiet and sweet content,
That it seems as if heaven to earth had lent
A part of its bliss.   And surely God meant
The homes of His people on earth to be
But a sweet foretaste of that home which He
Has in store for their blessed Eternity.
And so, when He enters their quiet abode—
His loved people they, and He their loved God
He reigns in that house and dwells in each heart,
And to every inmate doth always impart
Needed grace to support and uphold in his ways ;
Giving heed to their prayers, and accepting their
    praise.
Love reigns and Peace rules, and Hope never fails ;
For Faith in their Saviour at all times avails,
And triumphs o'er every foe that assails.

When we look upon such a sweet home as this,
And our hearts cry out, " Oh, whence all this bliss ? "
We answer, " The God who is working there,
Is He who hath made this world so fair."

There are places where prayer is wont to be made,
Where the little flock meet in the shelter and shade
Of Christ's loving presence, who meets with them there,
While His Spirit unburdens their hearts in the prayer
They unitedly pour in His listening ear,
And wait for the answer their faith makes them sure
He is waiting to grant, and abundantly pour
In blessing on all for whom they entreat,
In the time and the way which to Him may seem meet.
Oh, who can compute all the grace He imparts
At such meetings? The happy communion of hearts,
Knit together in love to each other and Him,—
Faith brightening their hope, which might erewhile be dim ;

The holy resolves and the blessèd delight,
Fresh courage obtained to endure, and to fight
The battle before them with self and with sin ;
With foes all around, and the traitor within.
They are girded anew for the conflict, and go
Forth still in His name and His strength, so they know
The victory certain over every foe ;
In that name and that strength they can't but o'ercome,
And in triumph ride on to the conqueror's throne.
Do we ask what's the secret of this power in prayer ?
He who made this fair world is still God working there !

Oh, how sweet are our Sabbaths, how sweet is their rest,
When, freed from our worldly work and its care,
We gather together, and meet as His flock,
With Himself in the midst, in His dear house of prayer.
We meet in His name, and we joyfully raise,
With our hearts full of love, our songs to His praise ;

At His footstool, in union, with one heart we bend,
And, with eager expectancy, hear and attend
With delight to the word it may please Him to send.

Oh, this is the place where He chooses to meet
With His people, and cheer them, as onward they go ;
'Tis here that He shows them His hands and His feet ;
'Tis here the bless'd waters of Siloam flow ;
'Tis here He unburdens the heart that o'erflows
With a love that no creature imagines or knows—
With a love such as none can declare or express,
Nor mortal nor angel can fathom the same ;
The Spirit, as promised, has come in His name
And the Father's—'tis He that alone can proclaim
Its height and its depth, and its breadth and its length,—
Almighty to save by its infinite strength !
'Tis here that He spreads, in this wilderness,
A table so furnished with viands divine ;
'Tis more than the food which His bright angels eat,
That His people find here in the bread and the wine ;

While their hearts, like His own, are made to o'erflow
With love such as none but His ransomed ones
    know ;
For to many a one has a Bethel been given,—
A house of God here, and a true gate of Heaven.
And we find that our Sabbaths and houses of prayer,
And all the true pleasures and peace we find there,
Are the gifts of that God we delight to declare
As the God who hath all of us under His care,—
Our own God, who for us made this bright world so
    fair !

REMINISCENCES.

"I have considered the days of old."—Ps. lxxvii. 5.

"Hear, ye children, the instruction of a father, and attend to know understanding. . . . He taught me also, and said unto me, Let thine heart retain my words."—Prov. iv. 1, 4.

SISTER, do you not remember,
    In our childhood's happy days,
How we round his knees would gather
And, to earn our father's praise,
Would recite the simple lays
We had learnèd; and what pleasure
It afforded, as, in measure
Soft and simple, grave or gay,
We found him hear what each could say?
Sweet psalms which our loving mother
Taught us, as she taught to pray,—

"The Shepherd Song," "The Exile's Wail,"
"Lone Bethel's God," "The Angel's Tale,"
"The Beggar Girl," "The Orphan Boy,"
"The Quarrelsome Dogs," "The Busy Bee,"
"All-seeing God," "Our Parents Dear,"
"Short Time and Long Eternity"—
  These were the subjects of our lays.
  Or, oft in concert with a brother,
  Short scenes from some well-chosen plays
  Would we enact, with flare and flutter;
  And sometimes, too, with stare and stutter,
  We'd stammer through our parts; and rage,
  And love, and wrath, and fight, and bluster,
  With all the skill that we could muster,
  Were shown upon our mimic stage.
  In Roman Senate we'd debate
  If peace or war should rule the State;
  Or to a Roman audience tell
  How basely their great Cæsar fell.
  I'd be Norval, he Glenalvon,
  Or 't might be the other way;
  And our mein, and tone, and gesture
  Start up before me at this day.

"The Soldier's Dream," "Lord Ullin's Daughter,"
"Beth-Gelert's Hound," "Glenara's Bride,"
"Young Lochinvar," "Culloden's Slaughter,"
"The Razor Seller," "Gilpin's Ride"—
  All these my memory recalls
  As spouted in these early days!

And one there was—I well remember—
That you had learnèd; and one day,
When visiting an aged neighbour,
In our loved father's company,
You were asked, and did repeat it.
'Twas a poet's tuneful lay,
Written to a mother mourning
O'er her firstborn, caught away
From the cradle where he lay.

Lately, in a pleasant volume,
I chanced on it; but it seemed
Sadly shorn, and but a shadow
Of the verses you had learned.

"Brother," interposed my sister,
"I remember well the lay
  That you speak of, and the day;

And though it's sixty years and more,
Yet, I think, I could repeat it
Even now, for in the store of
Memory all these years I've hid it."

So from line to line she said it,
Right fluently did it rehearse:
And you have it here, kind reader—
A gem amid my meaner verse.

TO A MOTHER ON THE DEATH OF HER FIRST-BORN SON.

Sleep, little baby, sleep—
Not in thy cradle bed,
  Not on thy mother's breast,
  Henceforth shall be thy rest,
But with the quiet dead.

Yes, with the quiet dead,
Baby, thy rest shall be.
  Oh, many a weary wight,
  Weary of life and light,
Would fain lie down with thee.

Flee, little tender nursling,
Flee to thy grassy nest;
   There the first flowers shall blow,
   The first pure flakes of snow
Shall fall upon thy breast.

Peace! peace!—thy little bosom
Labours with shortening breath.
   Peace! peace!—thy tremulous sigh
   Speaks thy departure nigh.
These are the damps of death.

I've seen thee in thy beauty,
A thing all health and glee,
   Yet never then wert thou
   So beautiful as now,
Baby, thou seem'st to me.

Thine upturned eyes glazed over,
Like harebells wet with dew,
   Already veiled and hid
   By their convulsive lid,
Their pupils darkly blue.

Thy little mouth half open,
Thy soft lips quivering,
 As if, like summer air,
 Ruffling the rose leaves there,
Thy soul were fluttering.

Mount up, immortal essence!
Young spirit, haste, depart!
 And is this Death? Dread thing,
 If such thy visiting,
How beautiful thou art!

Thou weepest, childless mother!
Ay, weep, 'twill ease thine heart.
 He was thy first-born son—
 Thy first, thy only one—
'Tis hard from him to part.

'Tis hard to lay thy darling
Deep in the damp, cold earth;
 His empty crib to see;
 His silent nursery,
Once gladsome with his mirth.

To meet again, in slumber,
His small mouth's rosy kiss;
   Then, wakened with a start
   By thine own throbbing heart,
His twining arms to miss.

To feel half conscious—why
A dull heart-sinking weight?
   Till memory on thy soul
   Flashes the painful whole,
That thou art desolate!

And then to lie and weep,
And think the livelong night!
   Feeding thine own distress,
   With accurate greediness,
On every past delight—

Of all his winning ways,
His pretty playful smiles,
   His joy at sight of thee,
   His tricks, his mimicry,
And all his little wiles.

Oh, these are recollections
Round mothers' hearts that cling,
    That mingle with the tears
    And smiles of after years,
With oft awakening.

But thou wilt then, fond mother,
In after years look back—
    Time brings such wondrous easing—
    With sadness not unpleasing,
E'en on this gloomy track.

Thou'lt say, " My first-born blessing,
It almost broke my heart
    When thou wert forced to go ;
    But yet for thee, I know,
'Twas better to depart.

" God took thee, in His mercy,
A lamb untasked, untried.
    He fought the fight for thee,
    He won the victory ;
And thou art sanctified.

"Now, as a dew-drop shrined
  Within a crystal stone,
    Thou'rt safe in heaven, my dove—
    Safe with the Source of love—
  The Everlasting One.

"And when the hour arrives,
  From flesh that sets me free,
    Thy spirit may await,
    The first at Heaven's gate,
  To meet and welcome me."

ASPIRATIONS.

"We know that, when He shall appear, we shall be like Him; for we shall see Him as He is."—1 JOHN iii. 2.

"And so shall we ever be with the Lord."—1 THESS. iv. 17.

WHEN the dead in Christ shall rise,
    Shall I be there?
When they see, with glad surprise,
The empty tombs, the opening skies,
    Shall I be there?

When He doth Himself appear,
    Shall I be there?
And they meet Him in the air,
Clothed, like Him, in raiment fair,
With garments such as angels wear,
    Shall I be there?

When He owns them as His own,
    Shall I be there?
Seats them with Him on His throne,
Lets them know as they are known,
    Shall I be there?

When they see Him as He is,
    Shall I be there?
And they wear a form like His,
Suited to the realms of bliss,
    Shall I be there?

When they hear the angels' song,
    Shall I be there?
When their glad notes they prolong,
Joining with the heavenly throng—
The choir to which they now belong—
    Shall I be there?

When they see the Father's face,
    Shall I be there?
Sinners saved from Adam's race,
Bright trophies of His wondrous grace,
Who now in His own home have place—
    Shall I be there?

When they're on the crystal sea,
    Shall I be there?
Gathering fruit from every tree,
That for the nations' healing be—
The tree of life to all now free—
    Shall I be there?

When He is Himself their light,
    Shall I be there?
Where there shall be no more night,
But ever-shining glory bright,
Such as ne'er met mortal sight,
And no darkness ere can blight,
    Shall I be there?

When as Shepherd He doth lead them,
    Shall I be there?
And in pastures green doth feed them,
Not a thorn there that could bleed them,
For from every ill He's freed them—
    Shall I be there?

Sharing in unending bliss;
Clothed with perfect righteousness;
Not a taint of sin remaining;
His strong arm for aye sustaining;
As our King for ever reigning;
Love, and peace, and joy abounding;
Angel-brethren us surrounding;
And, under His own care unfailing,
Universal love prevailing—
  Oh, shall I be there?

A DEATH-BED EXPERIENCE.

"Whom have I in heaven but Thee? and there is none upon earth that I desire beside Thee. My flesh and my heart faileth: but God is the strength of my heart, and my portion for ever."—Ps. lxxiii. 25, 26.

"THE foot of the cross, where my dear Saviour died,"
The dying one said, "is the place for me."
There is nowhere else where the sinner can hide;
But there's safety there, and there would I be.

Now, when this life's journey so soon will be o'er,
And I'll enter the dread eternity,
When I look behind, when I look before,

See sin in the past, in the future see
The Judge requiring account of me,
Of all I have done, of all I have been,
And an answer for all the sin He has seen;
When my mouth must be shut, and I, self-con-
    demned,
To His stern award and decree must bend—
Oh, I feel there is nowhere else I can hide,
Save the foot of the cross, where my Saviour died!

But glory be to Thee, my Lord and my God!
That, ere I go hence, Thou hast graciously showed
This refuge for sinners, appointed by Thee,
For such a poor, helpless, vile sinner as me.—
" For I'm just a poor sinner, and nothing at all;
But Christ is my Saviour, my all and in all!"

Long here have I lain 'neath Thy chastening hand,
And suffered much more than my friends under-
    stand:
They have felt for my sufferings, and lovingly sought
To lessen my pains, and all remedies brought
That skill and experience both could devise,
To conquer the sickness from which these arise.

But vain all the efforts their deep love inspire,
And all the kind nursing which nothing can tire !
Oh, how pleasing and soothing to me is their love,
And how I cling to them as round me they move ;
Yet though they so love me, and dearly are loved,
Oh, such Thy surpassing love, Saviour, I've proved,—
Were it said to me now, " Give up Jesus ; and then,
Delivered from all your diseases and pain,
And restored to all your dear loved ones again,
You'll live and be happy here all as before "—
I'd spurn the temptation. For, Jesus, oh, more,
Far more Thou art to me than husband or child,
So by such a temptation I'll not be beguiled ;
But all else I'll give up, my dear Jesus, for Thee,
And cling to the Saviour who died to save me.
I'll cling to Thee here, and I'll patiently wait
Till it please thee to come and to take me away ;
And the angels will carry me in by the gate,
Where other beloved ones to welcome me wait,
To be with Thee and them, and there evermore
    stay !

And as for the dear ones I'm leaving behind,
I can trust them, my Saviour, full gladly to Thee ;

And, I know, as I found Thee, they also will find
How precious a Saviour to all Thou can'st be.
Thou'lt seek them, and find them, and give them a place
Among those Thou hast ransomed, and be with them here;
Thou wilt lead them and guide them, upheld by Thy grace,
And Thou'lt bring them at last to be with me, where
There is no going out, and no parting is known;
But those who have hid 'neath Thy cross here below
Shall be kept in the home above near to Thy throne,
And—sickness, and sorrow, and suffering all gone—
Shall be filled with the bliss which the glorified know!

A BAIRN'S HYMN.*

"He shall gather the lambs with His arm, and carry them in His bosom."—Isa. xl. 11.

"Jesus called a little child unto Him. . . . . Despise not one of these little ones; . . . their angels do always behold the face of my Father which is in heaven."—Matt. xviii. 2, 10.

JESUS CHRIST loves little children;
 So does God the Father too:
There is nothing hated by Them
 But the naughty things we do.

And it vexes Them so sorely
 When They see us children sin;
For They know that wicked Satan
 Seeks to draw us then to him.

---

* *The late Dr. Guthrie, on his death-bed, asked those around him to sing him a "Bairn's hymn."*

But They watch o'er little children,
    And They hear our infant cries;
And, to keep us safe from Satan,
    Jesus to our rescue flies.

Then, whenever I feel naughty,
    To my Saviour-God I'll cry;
And His Spirit will come to me,—
    Nothing harms me when He's nigh.

He will make me good and gentle,
    Just like Christ Himself to be;
And I'll tell all how I love Him,
    For I know how He loves me!

THE COMPASSIONATE SAVIOUR.

"He beheld the city, and wept over it."—LUKE xix. 41.

"Daughters of Jerusalem, weep not for Me, but weep for yourselves, and for your children."—LUKE xxiii. 28.

"That repentance and remission of sins should be preached in His name, . . . beginning at Jerusalem."—LUKE xxiv. 47.

WHO is He, with piercèd hands
    Stretched out to us, still entreats
Rebel sinners, up in arms,
To turn to Him; and who weeps
As He sees them disregarding
His appeal, and offered pardon
Spurning from them with contempt?

Oh, 'tis Jesus! Who but Jesus
Thus with guilty man would bear?

Who but He would stand such treatment,
For such rebels still would care?
Truly His is love surpassing
All that ever we have known;
And such merciful compassion
By none other could be shown.

For them on the cross He prayed,
While they shed His precious blood,
And most freely them forgave,
As He prayed His Father would;
And, when risen from the grave,
This the sweet command He gave—
That, while the story of His grace
Be told to all in every place,
Such was His wondrous love to them,
He'd have His followers to proclaim
The joyful tidings in His name,
Beginning at Jerusalem!

Oh, who among us can withstand
The pleading of that piercèd hand?
Can still reject the offered grace,
And tell the Saviour to His face

That all the pains and pangs He bore,
And all the sufferings on Him laid,
Affects them not, or nothing more
Than tale forgot as soon as read?

Lord, if Thy sight of what our sin
Was bringing on us, moved Thy love,
So deeply Thy compassion raised,
And drew Thee from Thy throne above—
Should not the suff'ring Thou didst bear,
When hanging on th' accursed tree,
Show us how deep and vile our guilt,
When nothing but Thy blood thus spilt
From death and hell could set us free?
Should not Thy love to us thus shown
Attract our grateful hearts to Thee,
And bind us as our ears were bored
To door-post, Thine henceforth to be?

THE ALL-SUFFICIENT SAVIOUR.

"Jesus came and spake unto them, saying, All power is given unto Me in heaven and in earth."—MATT. xxviii. 18.

"If God be for us, who can be against us."—ROM. viii. 31.

"My grace is sufficient for thee: for My strength is made perfect in weakness."—2 COR. xii. 9.

WHY should disturbing doubts and fears,
    Perplexing, anxious thoughts intrude?
Let darkness flee, let light appear;—
    Our Jesus reigns—the Great, the Good!

Think of the countless myriad hosts
    Of living beings great and small;
'Twas He who made them, and 'tis He
    Who still provides and cares for all.

The angels that surround His throne,—
    The gnats that gambol in the air,
Alike display His wondrous power,
    Alike partake His constant care.

The mightiest of created ones
    Must bend to Him and own His sway;
The meanest that creation owns,
    Enjoy His care as much as they—

Then can He leave thee, or forget
    Who gives the meanest still their food?
No, perish such a sinful thought—
    Our Jesus lives—the Great, the Good.

How weak we are, how little strength
    We have t' uphold us in the fight;
We turn our backs upon our foes,
    And vainly safety seek in flight.

Sin strikes our weapons from our hands,
    Brings back again its bonds and chains;
Faith wavers, love is overthrown,
    And scarce a gleam of hope remains.

In such a case, what can we do,—
    O Jesus! what but flee to Thee?
I'm faint and famished, almost gone;
    Stretch forth Thy hand and rescue me.

Yes, Jesus! still with Thee is found
    Whatever helpless sinners need;
Thou'rt not a Saviour but in name—
Thou'rt everlastingly the same;
And all who ever to Thee came
Have recognised and own thy claim
    As Saviour of the lost indeed!

For fainting souls thou'lt still provide
    Abundant store of heavenly food.
We ne'er can fail, for Jesus lives
    And reigns as King—the Great, the Good!

FAINT AND WEARY.

"O Lord, I am oppressed; undertake for me."—Isa. xxxviii. 14.

"Hear me speedily, O Lord: my spirit faileth: hide not Thy face from me."—Ps. cxliii. 7.

"It is God that girdeth me with strength. . . . He teacheth my hands to war."—Ps. xviii. 32, 34.

OH, fain would I lay my burden down—
    My burden of battle and sin;
Oh, fain would I go where my loved ones have
    gone,
And flee to the refuge to which they have flown;
And I cry, while I lie here and helplessly groan,—
    "O Lord, take me in!—take me in!"

I've sleepless nights and I've weary days,
   The tempter's so dreadful a foe;
And I am so weak, I can scarcely raise
My feeble arm; and each struggle displays
Him strong and me weak; for his guileful ways
Perplex me so, that, in wild amaze,
My spirit looks up and despairingly says,—
   "O Lord, let me go!—let me go!"

"O faithless and doubting one!" Jesus cries,
   "Why send cries such as these to Me?
You are looking to self, giving heed to his lies
With whom you are fighting, forgetting your eyes
On Me should be fixed; for in no otherwise
   Can strength and peace come unto thee.

"I've blunted the weapons of this dreaded foe—
   Arise! and quit thee like a man;
I have girded thee fully from top to toe,
And with armour which I have tempered so,
That if you but use it now as you should do,
   And as those whom I strengthen can,—

"You'd quench all his fiery darts in your shield;
    You would pierce him through with your sword—
The sword which I erewhile against him did wield,
When of old I o'ercame and drove him from the
    field—
And now to the servant, all foiled, he will yield,
    As he did to the servant's Lord.

"Take up your weapons, and use them then,
    And cease in your folly to doubt;
For unbelief brings you but sorrow and pain,
And never can poor, weary sinners regain
Their peace and their joy, but by looking again
    To Him who at first brought them out
From the fearful pit and the miry clay;
And who, ever the same, will in no wise say
To any that trust Him, 'You're cast away!'"

"I WILL IN NO WISE CAST OUT."

"The word, . . . upon which Thou has caused me to hope."—Ps. cxix. 49.

"All the promises of God in Him are yea, and in Him Amen."—2 Cor. i. 20.

"Faithful is He that calleth you, who also will do it."—1 Thess. v. 24.

HE lies on his dying bed
   Wasted and thin;
But the darkness has fled,—
   The light has poured in.

He lies there in perfect peace—
   Vanished all doubt;
It was this brought the peace,—
   "I'll in no wise cast out."

Words by His lips spoken,
   Who once for us bled ;
And who never has broken
   A promise He made.

Oh, what more is needed
   To banish all fear,
Than such an assurance,
   So simple, so clear ;

And given by Him who hath
   Both power and will,
Whate'er He hath promised
   To all to fulfil?

Oh, then, let us trust Him
   Whatever our case :
There's none but may taste of
   The power of His grace.

We may trust in that here
   To support and sustain ;
For none that ere trusted
   Did trust Him in vain.

He will be with us still,
    As He's been in the past;
In Him we'll abide, and
    Oh, then at the last

He'll be with us in dying,
    And carry us through
The dark stream. When the city
    Bursts bright on our view,

He'll be there to receive us,
    While glad angels shout,
"Here's another brought home
    Whom He would not cast out."

GOD'S HOUSE ON EARTH.

"This is none other but the house of God, and this is the gate of heaven."—GEN. xxviii. 17.

"I was glad when they said unto me, Let us go into the house of the Lord."—Ps. cxxii. 1.

"Not forsaking the assembling of ourselves together, as the manner of some is."—HEB. x. 25.

OH, why is God's house by so many forsaken?
    They seem to forget that He meets with them there;
He has told us where two or three gather together,
    He is there, in the midst, both to speak and to hear.

Oh, did they but know how abundant the blessing,
    He waits there, on all who will take, to bestow,
What crowds there would then be, all eagerly pressing
    To share in His bounty—how gladly they'd go!

But alas! they don't know Him, for Satan deceives
    them,
    And draws them from Him and His worship
        away;
And they barter God's favour, and blessings eternal,
    For the world's fleeting pleasures that fade in a
        day.

Nay, Satan deceives them by calling them pleasures;
    They have sin in their root, and, apart from our
        God,
Then can end but in death—a meet ending for folly,
    Still choosing the evil, despising the good.

Oh, would they but listen to God's loving message,
    And hearken to Him who can never deceive,
He'd forgive all the past, He'd provide for the
    future,
    And shower on them blessings which they who
        receive

Would find blessings indeed, all others excelling,
    And so loudly calling for love and for praise,

That, with hearts overflowing, they'd flock to His
    dwelling,
  And joyfully there hymns of gratitude raise!

They would go to His house desiring to meet Him—
  With nothing but this would they rest satisfied;
And their hearts would rejoice, for to those who
    thus seek Him,
  We know His best blessings are never denied.

If so they would do, there'd be no more complaining:
  God's houses are empty, His worship despised;
But 't would seem as if He were again with us
    dwelling,
  And all the fond hopes of His saints realised!

We would say, with the Psalmist, such bright days
    foreseeing,
  As he looked with delighted heart, sharing the
    bliss,—
"Oh, bless'd are the people whose God is Jehovah;
  Yea, blessèd are they whom He owns to be His!"

INDEX TO SCRIPTURE TEXTS.

	PAGE
Genesis xxviii. 17,	160
,, xlii. 36,	14
Deuteronomy xi. 12,	41
Psalms xviii. 32, 34,	154
,, xxiii. 3,	86
,, xxiii. 4,	5
,, xxiii. 6,	113
,, xxxvii. 25,	113
,, lxxiii. 25, 26,	142
,, lxxvii. 5,	129
,, xc. 9,	113
,, xc. 12, 14,	118
,, cxviii. 14,	89
,, cxix. 18,	73
,, cxix. 28, 32,	49
,, cxix. 49,	157
,, cxxii. 1,	160
,, cxliii. 7,	154
,, cxlv. 9,	121
,, cxlv. 14,	41
Proverbs iv. 1, 4,	129
,, xxii. 20, 21,	78
Canticles i. 3,	8
Isaiah xi. 6,	96
,, xxxviii. 14,	154
,, xxxviii. 17, 19,	1
,, xl. 11,	146
,, lii. 7,	26
,, lviii. 13, 14,	38
,, lxv. 1,	26
Jeremiah xxx. 17,	86
Jonah ii. 9,	89
Micah vii. 8,	51
Zechariah ix. 17,	121
Malachi iii. 12,	41
Matthew i. 21,	8
,, xviii. 2, 10,	146
,, xxv. 23,	23
,, xxviii. 18,	151
Luke xiv. 16, 21, 28,	45
,, xviii. 16,	29
,, xix. 41,	148
,, xxiii. 28,	148
,, xxiv. 47,	148

	PAGE		PAGE
John vi. 37,	107	Galatians v. 6,	33
,, viii. 31,	64	Philippians i. 23,	76
,, ix. 25,	73	,, ii. 6, 7,	55
,, xiv. 26,	78	1 Thessalonians iv. 17,	138
,, xv. 8,	64	,, iv. 18,	18
,, xvii. 11, 12,	107	,, v. 24,	157
Acts vii. 59, 60,	11	1 Timothy ii. 5,	55
,, xv. 9,	33	Hebrews ii. 3.	89
Romans v. 1,	33	,, x. 25,	160
,, viii. 28,	14	,, xi. 14, 15,	58
,, viii. 31,	151	,, xi. 32,	33
1 Corinthians i. 27,	96	1 Peter i. 9,	33
2 Corinthians i. 3, 4,	18	2 Peter i. 1,	33
,, i. 20,	157	,, i. 14,	111
,, v. 8,	76	1 John iii. 2,	138
,, xii. 9,	151	,, v. 4,	33
Galatians iii. 26,	33	Revelation i. 18,	67

23rd Thousand, Price 1s. 6d.

"ONLY A SERVANT;"

OR,

A BRIEF MEMORIAL OF MARY H——,
BY AN ELDER OF THE CHURCH.

With Introductory Notice by the Rev. W. H. GOOLD, D.D.

ANDREW ELLIOT, *17 Princes Street, Edinburgh.*

Sold by all Booksellers.

In addition to the following selection from the Notices of the Press when the book first appeared, it has been favourably noticed and recommended by, among others—

The Rev. C. H. SPURGEON (in "*Sword and Trowel.*")
,, THOS. GUTHRIE, D.D., St. John's Free Church, Edinburgh.
,, J. R. MACDUFF, D.D. (Author of "The Faithful Promiser," &c.)
,, HORATIUS BONAR, D.D., Chalmers Memorial Free Church, Grange, Edinburgh.
,, JAS. ROBERTSON, United Presbyterian Church, Newington, Edinburgh.
,, GEORGE SMEATON, D.D., Professor of Divinity, New College, Edinburgh.
,, J. H. WILSON, D.D., Barclay Free Church, Edinburgh.
,, JONATHAN WATSON, Baptist Church, Duke Street, Edinburgh.

Notices of the Press.

"A striking, well-written, and most profitable memoir of a domestic servant."—*Christian Treasury*.

"There is certainly one good thing about the age we live in—the press supplies good matter for all and sundry, for high and low, for rich and poor, for kings and subjects, for parents and children, for masters and *servants*. Here, at least, is a very excellent little book for her who is 'only a servant.'... It is such a treatise as, under the Divine blessing, may not only make the good servant at home, but faithful servants of the Lord Jesus Christ. We therefore wish it a large circulation."—*London Weekly Review*.

"This is a singularly interesting narrative of a useful career in humble life.... The greater part of the volume consists of a Diary kept by Mary herself, which is wonderfully well written for one in her humble position.... Without going further into the merits of the book, we commend it very cordially to our readers; and it is particularly suitable for putting into the hands of servants. The title of the book is suggested by a phrase used by herself on her dying bed."—*Kelso Chronicle*.

"We have read this 'brief memorial' with much interest and pleasure. It records a few incidents in the life of an orphan girl, who spent the last five years of her life as nursery-maid in the writer's family; and contains extracts from her Diary, and some of her letters.... We have been surprised at the force and accuracy with which one who was 'only a servant,' and early left an orphan, expresses herself, and at the clearness with which she indicates to correspondents of her own rank the way of salvation. The book may be useful to many besides servants ; but we commend it specially as suited to young female servants."—*Evangelical Witness.*

"The volume is one which, when taken up, will compel the reader to go on until its last page. Though, in her own words, 'only a servant,' Mary H—— was a saint of God, of much simplicity and earnestness of character, and of no small amount of natural ability. Her journals are remarkable productions for one in her situation. The vigorous English in which they are written, as well as the piety they breathe, are certainly very striking, and show what the odd intervals of time well employed, what the sitting under an evangelical ministry, what divine grace, even in apparently adverse circumstances, can do to elevate the mind mentally and morally. The elder, who has written this memorial with great judgment, skill, and pious feeling, has rendered an important service to the Church of Christ."—*Reformed Presbyterian Magazine.*

"We beg to introduce the volume entitled 'Only a Servant—a brief Memorial of Mary H——, by an elder of the Church,' as exhibiting a most attractive picture of the ancient family simplicities, associated with, yet unperverted by, modern refinement, and what is still more impressive and instructive, sanctified and elevated by that fundamental equality of genuine Christianity which recognises no distinction between male and female, Greek or barbarian, bond or free, master or servant! The 'only a servant' was a remarkable character.... The volume is the finest commentary we have ever seen upon the 'Epistle to Philemon,' though, in all probability, the biographer was unconscious of making the least reference to that inspired letter.... It is written with power and skill, tenderness and sobriety."—*Fife Herald.*

"This little volume is a truly valuable addition to the literature of religious biography.... We have in abundance those of statesmen, soldiers, ministers, travellers, &c.... But here we have, in a brief touching narrative, the 'life' of a humble domestic servant, told by her master.... Noble in life, she was heroic in death; and she passed away after a brief, but severe illness, leaving behind her an example which, as recorded in this little unpretending volume, is worth a thousand sermons."—*Fifeshire Journal.*

"A brief but valuable sketch of one who (to use her own words) was 'only a servant,' but who was in the highest sense 'above a servant, a sister beloved' in Christ.... Her diary and letters, which are indeed very remarkable for one in her station, furnish evidence not only of the Christian principles under which she acted, but of the living communion which she maintained with Christ.... This little work is peculiarly fitted for presentation to servants."—*British Messenger.*

"Mary H——, was a servant girl of not more than twenty-eight years at her death, without a home other than the house in which for the time she served.... Yet was she a mature, intelligent, judicious, as well as devoted Christian, beautifully consistent in her personal walk, and fervently zealous in her endeavours to be spiritually useful to those with whom she was in any wise connected. Her writings, as here preserved, show, moreover, how cultivated a mind she had. The narrative of the dying scene is as touchingly beautiful as anything we have read for a long time."—*Brechin Advertiser.*

www.ingramcontent.com/pod-product-compliance
Lightning Source LLC
Chambersburg PA
CBHW022111160426
43197CB00009B/978